Book: Teach Yourself Adobe Dreamweaver CS6
Author: Niranjan Jha
Publisher: Cromosys Corporation
ISBN: Acquired
Date: January 2014
Category: Computer Education

Preface

Cromosys Publication's **Teach Yourself Adobe Dreamweaver** book is an optimal quality guide to the beginners and advanced learners of Dreamweaver. We are the leading eBook publisher of languages and technology. Our research and education center working for last fifteen years has made tremendous efforts to simplify the learning of Dreamweaver, and so we assure you that this book will walk you through in the simplest way in your entire course of learning, and will make you a master of this application in just one month of time. In Dreamweaver, you can create, design, test, and publish a website with all modern arts without having the necessity to learn any coding of HTML or CSS. The IT professionals all around the world are using this software for Web development. Being simple, precise, and complete, this book empowers you to get started with opening Dreamweaver to adding text, images, colors, templates, and testing the website. This manual offers its readers a cutting edge in Dreamweaver CS6 by providing step-by-step procedures and multiple illustrations, making this book an ultimate reference that you can use anytime and anywhere. This book is covered in such a way that it will be equally helpful to the novice users as well as the professionals. In starting, you will learn about the basic concept of Dreamweaver, then you will create a Web page setting its properties, and then you will insert text, graphics, hyperlink, and multimedia objects, such as Audio and Video in the Web page. You will also get aware of creating HTML objects, such as radio buttons and check boxes, Cascading Style Sheets (CSS), JavaScript, and Spry behavior. The lessons conceived and prepared by us will let you start learning from real basic making your move amazing, astonishing, and exhilarating for you. It's cool, simple, and sublime!

Niranjan Jha, the author of this and fifty other books published online, is the coiner, founder, and owner of Cromosys Corporation. His dedication in technological and linguistic research is significantly known to millions of people around the world. This book is the creation of his avowed determination to make the learning of Dreamweaver easy to the people. After you install the application on your system, you just have to follow the instructions of this book doing the same on your computer, and you will see that you are quickly learning everything. Just an hour of practice per day, and in a month of time you'll get a lot of knowledge, tips and tricks to work with this software. This is an unmatchable unique book of its kind that guarantees your success. The lessons are magnificently powerful to bring you into the arena of Web development. With the industrial growth from the year 2014, the accurate and profound knowledge of this software has influenced millions of minds; therefore we conceived the idea of making this book a guideline for those who want to be perfect in this application starting from real basic. What Dreamweaver does, no other software can do. It is the need of time that is why many people have been sharpening their knowledge to be good in it.

In the early days of World Wide Web, programmers and Web developers had to write lengthy code and check it for errors. The ever-increasing demand of websites led many software companies to rethink the entire process of creating websites, and they constantly looked for ways to create error-free and easy to update website quickly. This provided an impetus for the growth of specialized software for web development, such as ColdFusion, FrontPage, and SharePoint Designer, but Adobe's Dreamweaver won the race. In this powerful application you can use various Web technologies, such as Hypertext Markup Language (HTML), eXtensible Hypertext Markup Language (XHTML), Cascading Style Sheets (CSS), and JavaScript to create professional websites. Unlike HTML, you do not have to write lengthy codes in Dreamweaver to create any control on a Web page. You can view various elements of websites from the specific panels, such as INSERT, and drag those elements in the Design view of the Dreamweaver. It provides a graphical editing environment to develop websites, Web applications, and Web pages.

Cromosys, our languages and technology research and education center, saving human efforts from being wasted, is committed to help you gain profound and contemporary knowledge. The world growing with density has brought enormous opportunity to Web development talents irrespective of their geographical boundaries. We strongly believe that this book is useful for people working for Web creation, graphics and animation, media houses, and entertainment world. After you start the lesson, you don't need to worry about anything but just follow each and every step carefully. This book is designed to fulfill the instant need of learners in a very economical way, as it is easy to find on Internet and affordable to buy and share. Cromosys, our path-breaking pioneer training institute for Computer Courses, English Speaking, Mass Communication, Foreign Languages, and Competition Coaching, is dedicated to enlightening human mind with educational endeavors, and we are doing the same for last successful fifteen years. And recently we have come up with 'Worldwide Online Teaching System' for languages and technology. We not only hope but believe that your success is in your hand, as this book will take you miles ahead in your expectation. We always respect the views and comments of readers, so for any communication with regards to assistance, enquiry or collaboration, we are always there at your reach as it helps us improve our quality.

Niranjan Jha
Founder: Cromosys Corporation
Web: www.cromosys.in
               facebook.com/cromosys
Contact no.   +91-9561450045
Email address: cromosys@yahoo.com
Facebook link: www.facebook.com/niranjanjha1
Address: 001, Jaisatyam, Patankar Road, Nallasopara (W), Mumbai, India-401203.

Books by the same author: Teach Yourself Autodesk Maya, Teach Yourself Autodesk Combustion, Teach Yourself Autodesk 3ds Max, Teach Yourself Adobe Flash, Teach Yourself Adobe After Effects, Teach Yourself Tally, English Voice Accent and Pronunciation, Teach Yourself Spanish, Teach Yourself French, Teach Yourself German

Cromosys Corporation: Languages and Technology Research and Education | Books Editing and Publication | News Network and Film Production | Voice Art, Graphic & Animation Design | Web Development and Software Development | India and Overseas Education and Recruitment

Caution: All the writing works that include all the educational, non-educational books, novels, and articles of the author Niranjan Jha, are the registered contents of Online Digital Services and also published contents of his registered magazine FACE OFF - Inventing Truth, which carries registration no. MAHENG12112/13/1/2009-TC and the endorsement no. 3244 28/5/2009 with the Ministry of Information and Broadcasting, Govt. of India. Any plagiarism in this regard will attract strict legal action. Any further publication of any of his books requires his written permission.

Lesson 1
Introduction

Dreamweaver is the preferred choice for Web developers across the world because it has various advantages over other software used to create websites. Dreamweaver has a user-friendly interface, supports for different scripting languages, and is compatible with different software. It has a full-featured Web application development tool that helps you to create, modify, and manage a website. It is a What You See Is What You Get (WYSIWYG) interface, which you can use to add, view, and edit content in a Web page. The Dreamweaver interface also allows you to create HTML documents with the help of tools and panels that assist you in building your website. In Dreamweaver, you can work with HTML documents in three different modes: Design view, Code view, and Split view. In Design view, you work in Dreamweaver editor that displays the Web page almost as it will be seen in the Web browser window. You can insert elements, such as tables and images, and format them or drag them to place them in the Web page as desired. In the Code view, you can write code in HTML, CSS, JavaScript, and other languages as needed by the browser to display the webpage. In the Split view, the Document window is divided into two sections: Code view and Design view. This mode allows you to view the changes in the Code view and Design view simultaneously.

Features of Dreamweaver CS6

The latest version Dreamweaver CS6 offers several new features to create and design various interactive Web pages depending on your requirement. Some of the new and enhanced features of Dreamweaver CS6 are listed below:

Enhanced Content Management System (CMS): Provides a better authoring and testing support for the CMS frameworks, such as WordPress and Joomla. These frameworks allow you to build websites directly in the design view. In addition, the framework, such as WordPress, allows you to publish the content online and enables database integration.

Enhanced CSS inspection: Allows you to gain information about the relationships between various elements of the Web page, such as margins and padding, using the CSS inspect tool. The CSS inspection feature also allows you to quickly analyze the layout of the Web page by simply hovering over the desired Web page element.

New CSS Enable\Disable feature: Allows the interface to separate and temporarily disable different CSS rules while creating a website.

New Preview in Adobe BrowserLab feature: Helps you to test and preview the layout of the created Web page. Using the Preview in Adobe Browser Lab feature, you can also compare the Web page on different Web browser.

New Site Setup window: Allows you to quickly create a new website that does not consist of the scripting languages.

Multiple server support: Enables you to work with different servers during the website setup. For example, two server setup are present simultaneously, one for testing the server and another for testing a website.

Enhanced PHP code hinting: Provides you with the improvised support for PHP syntax, such as completion of code and syntax checking.

New Business Catalyst integration: Allows you to login to Business Catalyst (refers to an online service provided by Adobe) to perform synchronization of multiple websites simultaneously, using the Business Catalyst extension present in Dreamweaver.

Enhanced CSS starter pages: Refers to the improvised CSS starter pages that let you work with the created Web pages in a quick manner using the code provided by Dreamweaver. It helps you to create a website quickly.

Subversion: Refers to the feature used for maintaining and storing files and folders of previous versions for created website at a Subversion server, by tracking the changes when they are made.

Launching Dreamweaver CS6

You are going to launch Dreamweaver installed on your computer. In case you don't have the licensed copy of the software, you can download the trial version of the Dreamweaver software from the **https://www.adobe.com/cfusion/tdrc/index.cfm?product=dreamweaver&promoid=EBYEW** link. After installing Dreamweaver, select Start> All Programs> Adobe Dreamweaver CS6 to launch the application. First you see the launching splash screen, and then it shows the starting window of Dreamweaver as shown in picture 1.1.

Picture 1.1

The starting window of Dreamweaver consists of buttons to create new documents and open recent documents. The bottom pane of the starting window contains the buttons to connect to Adobe TV, Dreamweaver CS6 help, Dreamweaver Exchange, and resources.

Creating a New Web Page

After Dreamweaver application is launched, it opens the starting window that allows you to work with Dreamweaver document. The options in the starting window let you start creating a Web page. However, Dreamweaver gives you an alternate way to reach these options, and for that, you need to select the options available in the Menu bar of the Dreamweaver application window. For example, you can use the options available in the File menu to create a new document or open recent document. Dreamweaver provides you a flexible environment to work with a collection of different types of files. Apart from HTML documents, you can also create Active Server Pages (ASP), JavaScript, and CSS files. Perform the following steps to create a new Web page in Dreamweaver:

Teach Yourself Adobe Dreamweaver CS6 – By Niranjan Jha – Published by Cromosys

1. Select **File> New** from the Menu bar. It opens the <u>New Document</u> dialog box with the default settings on the screen.

2. Click the **Create** button in the New Document dialog box, as shown in picture 1.2 with a red arrow. This option is at the bottom right side. In this case, we will create a new Web page with the default settings. However, you can create a new document with the desired page type and its consequent layout, according to the requirement.

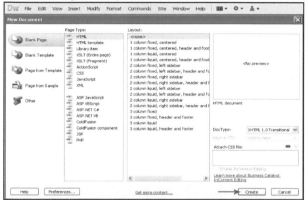

Picture 1.2

You will see that a blank Web page is created with the name **Untitled-1** in the Dreamweaver Application window, as shown in picture 1.3.

Picture 1.3

In the next section of the lesson, you are going to learn about the Dreamweaver interface and its various components.

Teach Yourself Adobe Dreamweaver CS6 – By Niranjan Jha – Published by Cromosys

Dreamweaver Interface

There are various panels, bars, and tools in Dreamweaver interface. These panels are used to create and manipulate the document. The interface is also called the Application window. The interface consists of the following components: the Application bar, the Document window, the PROPERTIES inspector, and the Panel group.

The Application Bar

In Dreamweaver, you can see the Application bar at the top of the Application window, as shown in picture 1.4. This is the very first bar of the Dreamweaver screen. This bar contains the Dreamweaver logo, the Layout dropdown list, the Extend Dreamweaver dropdown list, the Site button, the Menu bar, and the Workspace switcher.

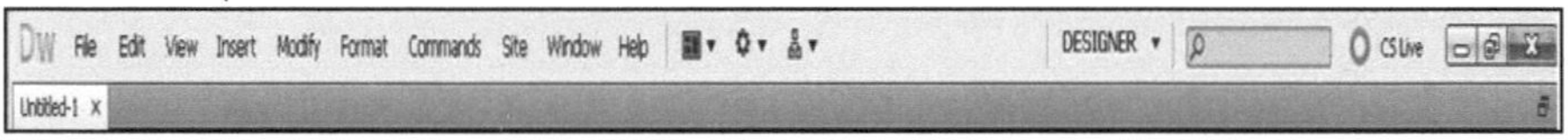

Picture 1.4

Now let us see in detail about the elements of the Application bar starting with the Dreamweaver logo at the left side.

The Dreamweaver logo: Minimizes, maximizes, or closes a Dreamweaver document. It is located at the left side of the Application window and displays a system menu when you click it.
The Layout dropdown list: Selects the Code and Design views. It is located beside Help option and provides options to select the layout of the document.
The Extend Dreamweaver dropdown list: Provides access to Extension manager, Web widgets, and other Dreamweaver extensions.
The Site button: Manages new Dreamweaver sites and edits existing ones.
The Workspace switcher: Toggles between the different workspace layout options.
The CS Live Services button: Allows you to interact with server-side applications and explore CS Live services, and helps in managing your Adobe BrowserLab account.
The Menu bar: Contains various menus, such as File, Edit, View, and Inspect to perform specific tasks. The menus are explained below:
The File menu: Helps perform basic operations in a Dreamweaver document, such as create, open, save, close, and import a document
The Edit menu: Modifies an existing document
The View menu: Changes the view settings of a document, such as zoom level and ruler guides
The Insert menu: Inserts images and tables in a Web page
The Format menu: Formats the text and objects present on a Web page
The Site menu: Creates new sites and manages existing ones
The Window menu: Performs various workspace-related tasks, such as opening a panel, creating a custom workspace, and managing the workspace

The Document Bar

The entire window where you can write the code is called the Document window. It is in the middle of the Dreamweaver screen. It is an area where you design a Web page. You can see this window below the Application bar. The Document window contains the Document toolbar and the text editor. The

Document toolbar provides buttons that allow you to toggle between the Code, Split, and Design views of a document quickly. In addition, the Document toolbar also contains some common commands and options for viewing the document and transferring it to the Local and Remote sites. The text editor allows you to edit code or insert elements to create a Web page. The picture 1.5 shows the Document window of Dreamweaver.

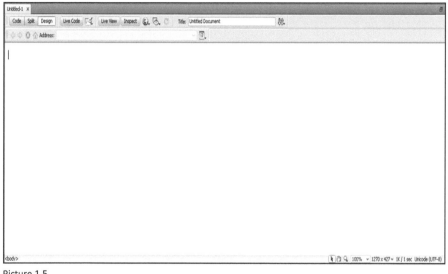

Picture 1.5

The PROPERTIES Inspector

You can see the PROPERTIES Inspector at the bottom of the Document window. This is the mostly used component of the Dreamweaver interface. It displays the properties, such as image, text, table, or frame, of the selected object in the window. If this panel does not appear on the Dreamweaver workspace, you can open it by selecting the Properties options from the Window menu.

The content of the PROPERTIES inspector varies and depends on the selected element. For example, if you want to change the size of an image, you can select the image and enter a new size for it in the PROPERTIES inspector. In the same way, buttons, list boxes, and text boxes in Dreamweaver have their own properties, which are displayed in the PROPERTIES inspector. The picture 1.6 shows the PROPERTIES inspector of a document in Dreamweaver.

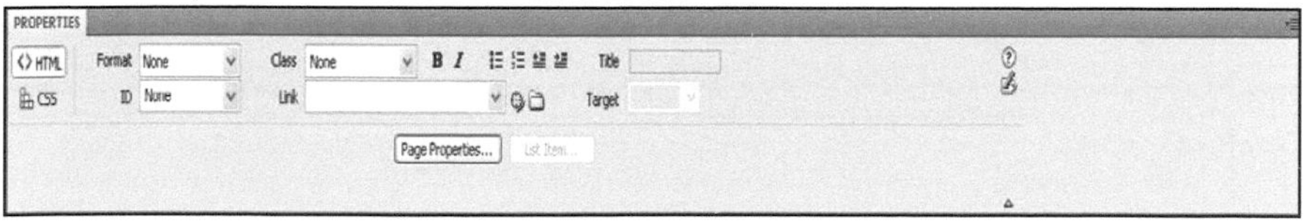

Picture 1.6

The Panel Group

A panel refers to a collection of tools that can be used to perform various operations related to a single task; whereas, a panel group represents a set of related panels that are tabbed in the dock. These panel groups can be collapsed or expanded and docked or undocked. The panels are displayed in the vertical orientation of the Dreamweaver workspace. The picture 1.7 shows the various panels of the Panel Group. It contains the panels, such as INSERT, CSS STYLES, AP ELEMENTS, FILES, and ASSETS. You are going to learn about all of these panels in the following sections. In case you accidently click off the Panel Group, you can get it back by clicking the option **CS Live** at the top right side, and then select **Adobe BrowserLab**. Then, you need to click Window tab at the top and enable **Insert**, and **CSS Styles**.

The INSERT Panel

You may need to double-click next to INSERT word to expand the INSERT Panel in the Panel Group. This panel is partly shown in picture 1.7. The INSERT panel contains buttons to insert different types of objects, such as images, tables, and links, in a document. Each object has an HTML code that allows you to set the various properties for it according to your requirement. For example, you can insert a table by clicking the Table button in the INSERT panel.

The CSS STYLES Panel

The CSS STYLES panel (also shown in picture 1.7), displays the name and other related information of CSS. It is a formatting technique that allows you to change the appearance of different items present on a Web page, such as text, heading, and images. The CSS STYLES panel contains a toggle button at the top that allows you to switch between two modes, the All mode and the Current mode.

In the All mode, the CSS STYLES panel displays two panes: the All Rules pane, which appears on the top, and the Properties pane, which appears at the bottom. The All Rules pane displays a list of rules defined in the current document as well as all rules defined in style sheets attached to the current document. The Properties pane allows you to edit CSS properties for any selected rule in the All Rules pane.

In the Current mode, the CSS STYLES panel displays the following three panes: (1) Summary for Selection: Displays the CSS properties for the current selection in the document. (2) Rules: Displays the location of selected properties. (3) Properties: Allows you to edit CSS properties for the rule applied to a selection.

Picture 1.7

The AP ELEMENTS Panel

The AP ELEMENTS (absolutely positioned elements) panel manages the AP elements in a document. It can be accessed by clicking the tab beside the CSS STYLES tab. An AP element in Dreamweaver is an HTML page element, normally a <div> tag that has an absolute position assigned to it. The AP ELEMENTS panel helps to prevent overlapping of AP elements. It also allows you to change the visibility of AP elements, nest or stack AP elements, or select one or more AP elements. These elements are displayed as a list of names, and the AP element that is created first appears at the top of the list.

The FILES Panel

The FILES panel (also shown in picture 1.7), organizes the files for your Dreamweaver sites and provides the features needed to manage the files. Using the FILES panel, you can create new files and folders, open existing files, copy, delete, rename, and move files. The FILES panel manages both local and remote sites. You can view and manage files in both sites, as well as transfer files from one site to the other.

The ASSETS Panel

The ASSETS panel helps you to manage and organize assets, which are elements, such as images and media files. It can be accessed by clicking the tab beside the FILES tab. You can also drag the assets to the Document window from the ASSETS panel, and use them in your Web page.

Lesson 2
Working with the Document Window

You have already learnt that a document can be viewed in the various modes, such as Code view, Design view, and Split view. Before making any changes to a document, you need to select a mode according to your requirement and convenience. The mode allows you to view the page as you want. The following sections will explain the different modes to view and work on the Dreamweaver workspace.

Opening the Document in the Code View

The Code view is a viewing option that allows you to view the code related to a Web page. Using the Code view of the document, you can also write your code and edit the existing code. You can open a document in the Code view by selecting **View> Code** from the View menu in the Menu bar. You can open it once to see how it looks.

Opening the Document in the Split View

The Split view is a viewing option in which you can view a document in dual mode. When you select the Split view option, the document appears in the Code view along with the Design view. You can open a document in the Design view by selecting **View> Code and Design** from the View menu. Try to open it once to see how it looks.

Opening the Document in the Design View

The Design view option allows you to view your Web page graphically. It is very easy to work in the Design view as you can insert an object simply by selecting the object and dragging it onto the page. You can open a document in the Design view by selecting **View> Design** from the View menu. Open this view also to see how it looks.

Working with the Workspace

When we talk about workspace, it means an area containing the various options, such as panels and buttons that are necessary to design a document. There are also certain preset workspaces, such as Designer, Classic, Coder, Dual Screen, and App Developer. The panels and tools in the preset workspace are arranged according to its theme. But when you work on a project, you can customize a workspace as per your requirement. You can perform various tasks on a workspace according to the requirement of the user, such as opening different workspaces, creating a new workspace, and managing the workspace. Now we will discuss about these tasks one by one.

Opening a Different Workspace

At the time of starting the Dreamweaver application, the DESIGNER workspace appears by default on your screen. But for your convenience, Dreamweaver allows you to open another workspace or create a workspace of your own. Let us perform the following steps to open a different workspace:

1. Click the workspace **switcher** list box in the Application bar, as shown in picture 1.8 with a red arrow. It displays a dropdown list.

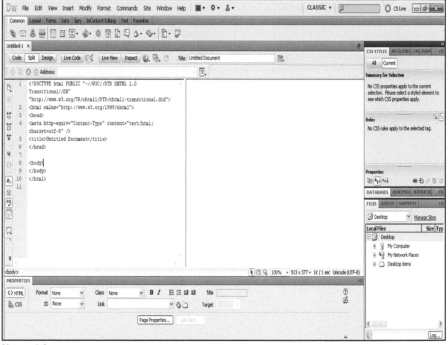

Picture 1.8

2. Select the required workspace from the dropdown list. For now, you can select **Classic** workspace. The Classic workspace theme is applied to the Application window, as shown in picture 1.9.

Picture 1.9

Creating a New Workspace

Dreamweaver allows you to create your own workspace by rearranging the position of panels in it. After repositioning the panels, you can save that workspace as your default workspace. Perform the following steps to create a new workspace:

Teach Yourself Adobe Dreamweaver CS6 – By Niranjan Jha – Published by Cromosys

1. **Arrange** the Dreamweaver workspace as per the requirement. In our case, we have collapsed all the panel groups to icons, as shown in a red rectangle in picture 2.0. In this picture the red arrow indicates the collapse button.

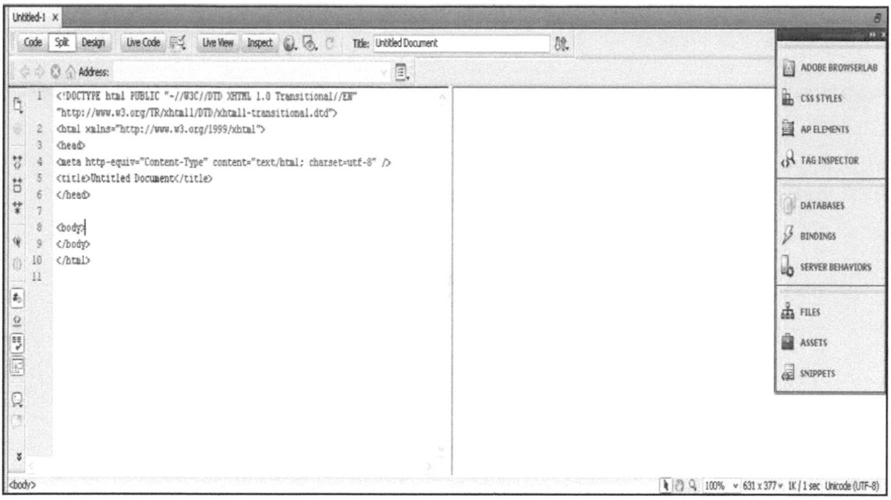

Picture 2.0

2. Click the **Workspace switcher** list box in the Application bar. Then, select the **New Workspace** option from the dropdown list. It opens the New Workspace dialog box.

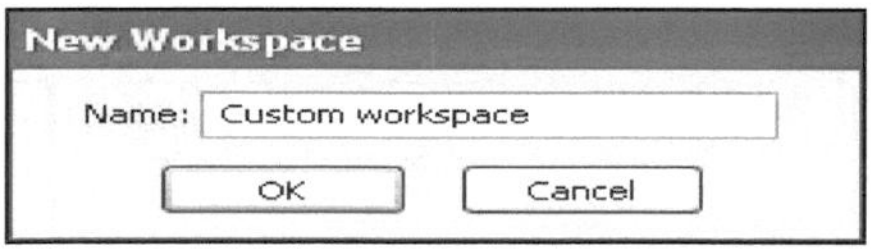

3. Type the name of the workspace in the <u>Name</u> text box. For now, you can type the name as **Custom workspace** (shown in picture 2.1). Then, click **OK** button to save the workspace with the name you typed.

Picture 2.1

The workspace is saved with the name Custom workspace and you can see it now in the <u>Workspace switcher</u> box.

Managing a Workspace

You have learnt to create a workspace, and then save it for future use. But after you save a workspace, you can manage the workspace by making changes to it anytime, deleting the workspace or renaming the workspace. In this section, you will learn to rename the workspace that you have created in the preceding section. Perform the following steps to manage (rename) a workspace:

1. Click the **Workspace switcher** list box in the Application bar, and select the **Manage Workspace** option from the dropdown. It opens the Workspace dialog box.

2. Select the name of the workspace that you want to rename. For now, you can select **Custom workspace**.

3. Click the **Rename** button at the right side in the Manage Workspace dialog box. The Rename Workspace dialog box appears.

4. Type the required name of the workspace in the Name text box. For now, you can type the name as **Random workspace**, and click **OK**.

5. Click **OK** button in the Manage Workspace dialog box. The Manage Workspace dialog box closes and the workspace appears with the modified name as **Random workspace**.

Saving a Web Page and Quitting the Application

At the time of saving the HTML document, there are certain conventions to follow. Some of these conventions are listed below:

- You should not use special characters, such as hash (#) and apostrophe (') in the name. For example, you should not name a Web page with an apostrophe, such as Mysite's.html.

- You can use underscore (_) or hyphen (-) to separate the words in the name. For example, My_Site.html is a correct name.

- You can name the main page (or the home page) of your website as index.html or home.html, depending on your Web server. Some Web servers are set up to handle home.html, or default.asp for dynamic sites, but most commercial service providers serve index.html before any other page in any folder on a site.

Dreamweaver automatically adds the .html extension to the end of the name of an HTML document. In case you want to change the extension of the document, you can use the Preference option available in the Edit menu. After saving the changes you made in a document, you can close the document. The content of the document remains unchanged until you open the document again and make changes to it. Now let us perform the following steps to save the HTML document and quit the application:

1. Select **File> Save** from the Menu bar of your Dreamweaver screen. It opens the Save As dialog box where you can enter the information of the document.

2. **Browse** to the location from the Save in list box where you want to save the HTML document. It is advisable that you should have a folder created with the name Dreamweaver CS6 on your hard drive, in which you can save all the documents.

3. **Type** the name of the HTML document in the File name text box. For example, you can type the name as **People Welfare**, and click the **save** button in the Save As dialog box.

The HTML document is saved with the name **People Welfare.html**. After saving the HTML document, you can further add content, such as text and images, to create a Web page. When you have completed your work, you can quit the application by selecting **File> Exit**.

Teach Yourself Adobe Dreamweaver CS6 – By Niranjan Jha – Published by Cromosys

Lesson 3
Working with a Website

From this lesson, you are going to work with a website. At this point, you need to know that Dreamweaver is a Web editor that allows you to design and develop a website. And a website is a collection of Web pages that contains several elements, such as text, special characters, graphics, hyperlinks, and email links, to represent information. In Dreamweaver you create customized websites by using the Site Setup dialog box. This dialog box allows you to set the information of your website, such as name of the website, the path to the directory where the files of the website are stored, and the Uniform Resource Locator (URL) of the website. To support the development process, you create a Dreamweaver website in three different folders: Local, Remote, and Testing Server. In most cases, you create and edit your Web pages in the Local folder on your computer, and then, when your website is completed to your satisfaction, you copy the Web page files to the folder where the users can access your website. A brief description of the types of website is mentioned in the following sections.

Analyzing Static and Dynamic Websites

You have understood that a website is a collection of inter-related Web pages that provides you information, such as products or services. Websites can be broadly categorized into two types: static and dynamic.

Static websites refer to a collection of Web pages that are created using Hypertext Markup Language (HTML) only, and the content present in these Web pages does not change frequently. These websites are designed on a small scale and for the entities that provide static information, such as Wikipedia. Static websites are easy to develop, build, test, and publish on a Web server; however, the websites are expensive to update and the content in the Web pages can become stagnant.

In dynamic websites, such as websites used for e-commerce, content is refreshed very frequently. The dynamic websites gather information from different sources and create Web pages dynamically on a Web browser. These Web pages are created using different programming languages, such as Cascading Style Sheets (CSS), Extended Hyper Text Markup Language (XHTML), or Hypertext Preprocessor (PHP). Different combination of these programming languages serves helps automate the website. In addition, dynamic websites provide advantages, such as updated content and interactivity.

Understanding Website Structure

Before creating a website, you should first define the structure of a website in Dreamweaver for optimum and efficient utilization of the features of Dreamweaver. To define the structure, you first need to set up a Local folder. After a Local folder is set, you must add all the information related to a website in the Remote and Testing Server folders to transfer files on a Web server for developing the website. The structure of a website created using Dreamweaver consists of the following three folders:

Local: Contains all the files, images, and other assets of a website, you are working on. Dreamweaver refers to this folder as a Local site. The location of this folder can be your local computer or a network server. The Local folder is also known as the Root folder.

Remote: Stores all the Web pages created for testing, production, and collaboration. The Remote folder has the same name as the Local folder because your Remote folder is usually an exact duplicate of your Local folder. That is, the files and subfolders that you post to your Remote folder are copies of the files and subfolders that you create in the Local folder.

Testing Server: Specifies the location where you want your dynamic Web page to be processed. In other words, Testing Server folder is an alternative location where you can test your files on a server with an identical database setup, without deploying the files to the live website while they are still under development. The testing server can also be on your local computer.

Organizing the Root Folder

After you have set up a Local folder, you need to decide the structure of a website, such as establishing hyperlinks between Web pages. Each Web page of a website has its own unique address known as the URL, such as www.yahoo.com. When you make a local hyperlink (a hyperlink from one Web page to another on the same website), you do not need to specify the complete URL of a Web page; instead, you just need to set the relative path (a path from a Web page to the linked Web page). The following are the three types of hyperlinks path used in Dreamweaver:

Absolute path: Provides the complete URL for linking the Web page, including the protocol to use (usually http:// for Web pages). A generic absolute path is as follows:
Protocol name://website name/path/file name
For example: http://www.adobe.com/Project/index.html. You must use an absolute path to link to a Web page on another server.

Document-relative path: Links a Web page to another Web page either in the same folder or in another folder by defining the path through the folder hierarchy from the current document to the linked document. If the path of the current Web page and the linked Web page is same, then the document-relative path excludes the same path of the Web pages. However, if the path of the current Web page and the linked Web page is different, then the document-relative path provides only the portion of the path that differs. This path is mainly used for local hyperlinks on a website. These hyperlinks are particularly useful when the current Web page and the linked Web page are in the same folder. A generic document-relative path is:
"common folder name/file name"
For example: <img src="images/title.gif">.

It is important to say that in the preceding example, there is no need to write the URL of the image you are linking, as both the images contain the same URL.

Site root-relative path: Defines the path from the website's root Web page to the linked Web page. This hyperlink path is useful either when you work on a large website that uses several servers, or when one server hosts several websites. The root-relative path is similar to the document-relative path; however, you need to add a forward slash (/) at the beginning of the path.
For example: <img src="/images/title.gif">.

It is important to say that in case you frequently move the HTML files from one folder to another, then you should use site root-relative path for hyperlinks.

Setting Page Properties

You can modify the properties, such as background color, margins, hyperlink styles, font size, and color, of different elements of a Web page with the use of Page Properties dialog box. The customized settings that you set are applied only to the current page. If you are using an external CSS, then you cannot apply the customized settings on a Web page, as Dreamweaver does not overwrite the tags set in the style sheet. Now you can go ahead and perform the following steps to set the properties of a Web page in Dreamweaver:

1. Select **Modify> Page Properties** from the Menu bar. It opens the Page Properties dialog box on the screen.

2. Select the type of Web page that you want to customize from the Category section on the left side. For now, you can select the **Appearance (HTML)** option, as shown in picture 2.2 indicating with a red arrow.

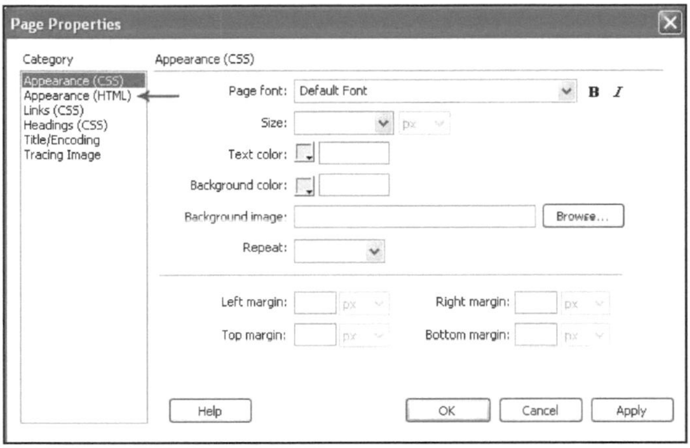

Picture 2.2

The Appearance (HTML) page appears in the Page Properties dialog box. In this page, you can set the desired properties, such as background color and background image. For now, we are modifying the background color of a Web page.

3. **Click** the down arrow of the Background color box to select the desired background color. The fly-out menu appears.

4. **Select** the desired color that you want to set as a background color. You can select purple color in this case, and **click** OK button to set the background color of the Web page. You will see on your screen that the background color of the Web page changes to purple.

Creating a Website

You may like to know that Dreamweaver helps you to place your Web page on Internet Explorer. Creating a Dreamweaver website refers to organizing all the Web page associated with a website. In Dreamweaver, a website can be created by using the Site Setup dialog box, which consists of the following tabs:

Site: Allows you to specify the name for your website and the name of the Local folder in which you want to keep all the website's files.

Servers: Allows you to select the server that is used to host the Web pages over the Web. Specifying values for this section is not mandatory, since the website can also be created without being published on the Internet.

Version Control: Allows you to access the Subversion settings, such as tracking the changes made to the files of the created website.

Advanced Settings: Allows you to perform functions related to a website, such as defining a website's production, collaboration, and deployment capabilities. Perform the following steps to create a website using the Site Setup dialog box:

1. Select **Site> New Site** from the Menu bar. It opens the <u>Site Setup for Unnamed Site 2</u> dialog box on your screen, as shown in picture 2.3.

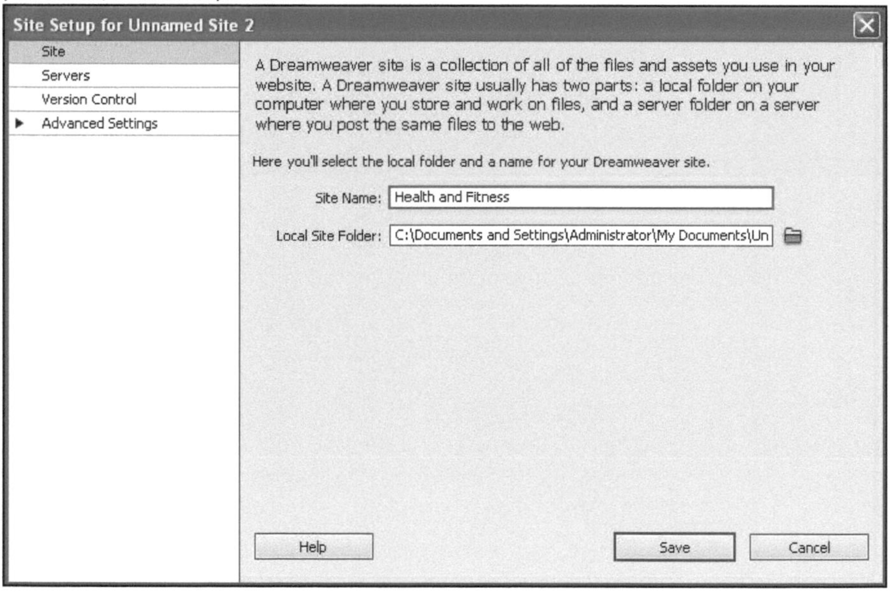

Picture 2.3

2. **Type** the name of website in the <u>Site Name</u> text box. In this case, you can type the website name as **Health and Fitness**.

3. **Click** the <u>Browse for folder</u> button to set the Local folder where you want to keep all the files of the website. It opens the <u>Choose Root Folder</u> dialog box.

4. **Browse** to the location of the <u>Root folder</u> from the <u>Select</u> list box. In this case, the location is **Dreamweaver CS6 folder** that you have already created on your hard drive.

Picture 2.4

5. Click the **Select** button in the Choose Root Folder dialog box. The selected location is added to the Local Site Folder text box below the Site Name option (shown in picture 2.3).

6. Click the **Save** button at the end. You will see that the Health and Fitness website is added in the **FILES** panel. The picture 2.4 is showing this website added in the FILES panel.

After creating the website, we need to learn different skills to manage it. The next section, the Website Managing Skills will explain you everything in detail.

Website Managing Skills

While creating or editing a website, sometimes you find that you have included incorrect information in the website. In such case, you can create a duplicate copy of your website for future reference and make necessary changes in the original website. You can also delete the website in case you no longer need it. In addition, you can manage your website by exporting it to a different location. In this section, you learn to create a duplicate copy of a website, delete a website, and export a website.

Duplicating a Website

Dreamweaver allows you to create duplicate copies of an existing website using the Duplicate button present in the Manage Sites dialog box. Dreamweaver copies all the settings (the settings specified at the time of creating the website) and creates a new website with the same filename appended with the text, copy. In other words, Dreamweaver does not copy the actual files; rather, it just creates a new website that can be manually modified. The copied website appears in the site list of the Manage Sites dialog box. Perform the following steps to duplicate a website:

1. Select **Site> Manage Sites** from the Menu bar of Dreamweaver screen. It opens the Manage Sites dialog box.

2. Select the website that you want to duplicate from the Manage Sites dialog box. For now, you can select the **Health and Fitness** website.

3. Click the **Duplicate** button in the Manage Sites dialog box. The duplicate copy of the Health and Fitness website with the name, **Health and Fitness copy** is added in the Manage Sites pane. Click the **Done** button in the Manage Sites dialog box at the end.

Deleting a Website

You can also remove a website from the list of websites. However, the website and its related information are not removed; they remain present in your computer so that you can retrieve and use this information whenever required in future. Perform the following steps on your computer to delete a website:

1. Select **Site> Manage Sites** from the Menu bar. Then select the website that you want to delete from the Manage Sites pane. For now, you can select the **Health and Fitness copy** website.

2. Click the **Remove** button in the Manage Sites dialog box. Then click the **Yes** button in the message box that prompts you to confirm the deletion.

3. Click the **Done** button in the Manage Sites dialog box to close. In the next section, you will learn to export a website.

Exporting a Website

Dreamweaver allows you to export a website which is a very good option in it. The professional Web developers need to export the websites while they are editing. When you want to work on your website using a different computer then you need to recreate the website with the same settings and copy the Web pages from your previous computer to the new computer. However, Dreamweaver helps you to save and reopen websites as eXtensible Markup Language (XML) files by using the Import and Export features. You can export a website with all its settings as an XML file to the desired location and use it on another computer or the same computer, depending on your requirement. Perform the following steps to export a website:

1. Select **Site> Manage Sites** from the Menu bar. Then select the website that you want to export from the Manage Sites pane. In this case, you can select the **Health and Fitness** website.

2. Click the **Export** button in the Manage Sites dialog box. It opens the Export Site dialog box on your screen.

3. Now you should have a folder with the name **Samples** created in your hard drive. Then, **browse** to the location of the Samples folder from the Save in list box in Export Site dialog box.

4. Click the **Save** button to save the file. The website is exported to the Samples folder with all its settings as an XML file that you can use on another computer or the same computer.

Lesson 4
Working with Web Pages

Dreamweaver is a Web editor that allows you to design, develop, and manage complex Web pages. You can create a Web page in Dreamweaver by simply dragging and dropping objects into the documents and formatting properties of the objects using the PROPERTIES inspector. Dreamweaver also provides support for Web technologies, such as JavaScript, and various server-side scripting languages and frameworks including ColdFusion and JavaServer Pages.

Using Dreamweaver, you can insert various elements, such as text, images, or hyperlinks, in a Web page according to your requirements. Insertion of different elements makes the Web page alluring by breaking its monotony. For example, consider a Web page that consists of text, which is unaligned, written in continuous form without any space or breaks. The Web page would look dull as compared to a Web page that is properly aligned with insertion of breaks, images, and hyperlinks at appropriate places.

Teach Yourself Adobe Dreamweaver CS6 – By Niranjan Jha – Published by Cromosys

Working with Text

In Web world, text is the best medium to represent information. The two main aspects of text in a Web page are the structure and presentation of the text. The arrangement of text using the necessary elements, such as paragraph, heading, and lists, is called the structure of the text. The final appearance of text using the elements, such as font face, text color, and size is called the presentation of the text.

Adding Text

Dreamweaver works like a word processing program, such as Microsoft Word. When you create a new document in Dreamweaver, the blinking cursor appears at the top left corner of the page where you can type text. You can add text by typing it in the Document window of the Dreamweaver application. As you type the text, it automatically wraps to the next line when it exceeds the right margin. Let us perform the following steps to add text in a Web page:

1. **Create** a new Web page selecting File> New> Create. Then **save** this Web page with the name **Articles.html** in the Dreamweaver CS6 folder on your hard drive.

2. **Type** the following text in the Articles.html Web page that you created, making sure the text is typed exactly the same (managing spaces):

Health Benefits

Regular exercise can help protect you from heart disease and stroke, high blood pressure, noninsulin-dependent diabetes, obesity, back pain, osteoporosis, and can improve your mood and help you to better manage stress. For greatest overall health benefits, experts recommended that you do 20 to 30 minutes of aerobic activity three or more times a week and some types of muscle strengthening activity and stretching at least twice a week. You can also include the following tips in your daily routine for a healthy life:

Drink lots of Water
Include variety of fruits in your daily diet
Avoid junk food
Avoid caffeine products in large amount
Have a handful of nuts as snack, especially in the winter season
Meditate and spend sometime only for yourself

Setting Text Properties

In Dreamweaver, setting text properties refers to setting text value. The text properties define the appearance and arrangement of the text in the Web page. In Dreamweaver, you can use the PROPERTIES inspector to set the properties of the text. The PROPERTIES inspector is divided into two sections: HTML PROPERTIES inspector and CSS PROPERTIES inspector. Perform the following steps to set the text properties:

1. **Enable** Design view of the Articles.html document on your screen by selecting View> Design from the View menu.

2. **Select** the text heading "Health Benefits" by dragging the cursor over it, and click the **CSS button** in the PROPERTIES inspector. The PROPERTIES inspector is at the bottom of the Dreamweaver screen (already shown in picture 1.6). The CSS PROPERTIES inspector displays various CSS properties.

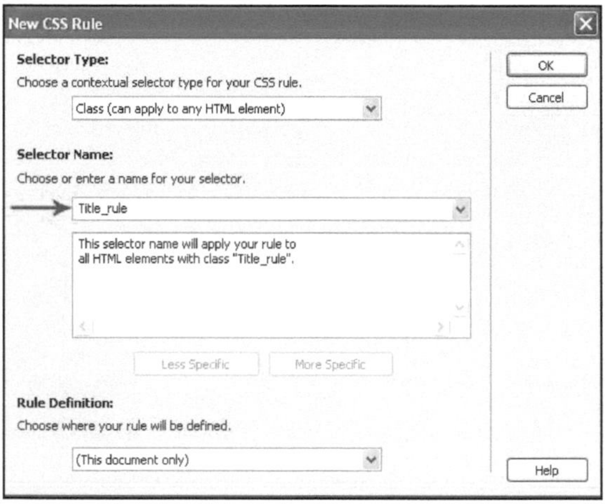

3. Click the down arrow of the **Size** combo box in the CSS PROPERTIES inspector. It opens a list of different font sizes. You need to select the font **size 24** from the list. It will open the New CSS Rule dialog box, as shown in picture 2.5.

4. Type the name: **Title_rule** under the Choose or enter a name for your selector list, as shown in picture 2.5. This way, you specify the name of the selector to define the CSS rule. Then, click **OK** button in the New CSS Rule dialog box. You will notice that the CSS rule is added to the Targeted Rule list box and the size of the text is changed to 24 px.

Picture 2.5

5. Click the **Align Center** button in the CSS property pane. It will align the text "Health Benefits" to the center position.

6. Click the **Color** down arrow in the CSS property pane, and select the **blue** color. You will see that the color is applied to the selected text. You can set the text properties of other text in the document in the same manner as you have set the text property of the heading.

7. Now to set the text properties of other text, click the **<HTML>** button in the PROPERTIES inspector which is above the CSS button. This option is shown in the picture 2.6 with a red arrow. Keep in mind that Dreamweaver provides two sets of properties to format the text: HTML properties, and CSS properties.

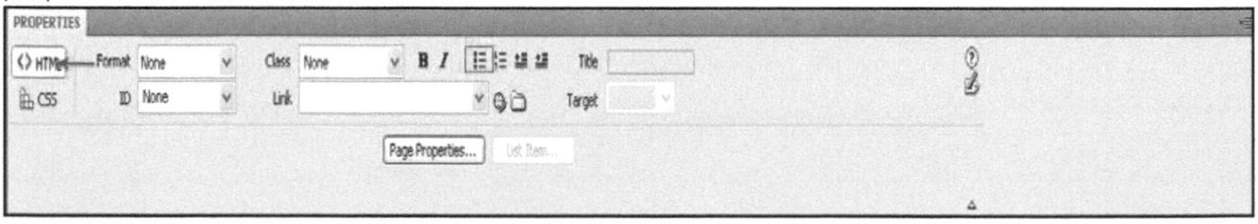

Picture 2.6

8. **Select** the health tips (all six lines from the bottom) in the document. Then click the **Unordered List** button, as shown in picture 2.6 in a red rectangle. The bulleted list is applied to the health tips. In case the bullet is not applied, you need to press Enter at the end of every line.

So you have created this Articles.html Web page in your Health and Fitness website. Your Web page Articles.html should look as shown in picture 2.7. You can also view this Web page in Internet Explorer by double-clicking Articles icon in Dreamweaver CS6 folder of your hard drive.

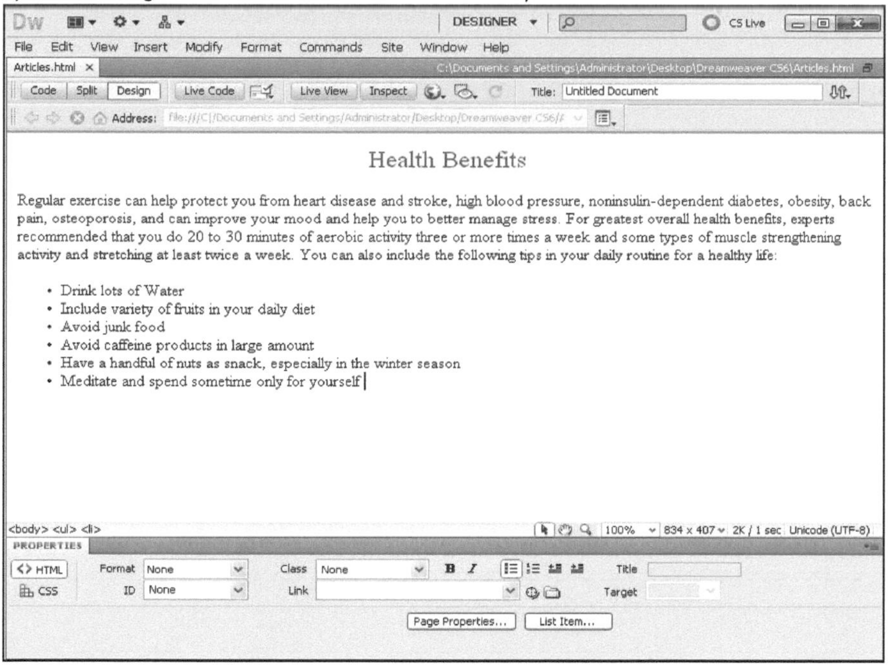

Picture 2.7

HTML Properties

You can use the HTML PROPERTIES inspector to make structural changes in the text present on a Web page. You can set various properties of the text, such as paragraph, heading level, and title by using the HTML PROPERTIES inspector. The following are the options available in the HTML PROPERTIES inspector:

Format: Sets the paragraph style and heading level of the selected text.

ID: Assigns and ID to the selected text.

Class: Displays the class style currently applied to the selected text.

Bold: Sets the font style of the selected text as bold.

Unordered List: Allows you to create a bulleted list for the desired text.

Ordered List: Creates a numbered list of the selected text.

Blockquote: Applies the <blockquote> HTML tag or block quotation to the paragraph, list, or block of text.

Remove Blockquote: Removes the <blockquote> HTML tag or block quotation from the paragraph, list, or block of text.

Link: Creates a hyperlink on the selected text.

Title: Specifies the textual tooltip for the hyperlink text.

Target: Specifies the name of a frame or window. The name of a frame or window is used as target container in which the document actually loads in the Web page. For example, frame 1 in a Web page could be used as Target to display some SWF (Shock Wave File) which is created in Adobe's Flash software.

Page Properties: Opens the Page Properties dialog box, where you can modify the properties, such as default font face, background color, and margin spacing of the currently open page.

CSS Properties

The CSS PROPERTIES inspector is used to set the presentation style of the text, such as its color, font face, font style, and size. You can set the CSS properties of the text from the PROPERTIES inspector. The following options are available in the CSS PROPERTIES inspector:

Targeted Rule: Adds new rule, applies a CSS class, and removes a CSS class from the selected text.

Edit Rule: Allows you to open the CSS Rule Definition dialog box. You can use the CSS Rule Definition dialog box to specify rules for the target. For example, you can change to font-face, color, and size of the text by using the CSS Rule Definition dialog box.

CSS Panel: Allows you to open the CSS STYLES panel and view the properties of the targeted rule in the Code, Design, or Split view.

The other options in the CSS PROPERTIES inspector are self-explanatory.

Inserting Special Characters

Special characters are characters other than numerals (0-9) and letters (A-Z). The examples of special characters are ©, !, @, #, $, %, ^, &, *, and ®. Perform the following steps to insert special characters in the **Articles.html** Web page:

1. **Click** at the bottom of the document to insert the special character. Then select **Insert> HTML> Special Characters> Copyright** from the Menu bar. The Copyright symbol is inserted at the selected place in the document.

2. After the Copyright symbol, **type**: All rights reserved. It will complete the sentence on the document. In the next lesson, you will learn to insert images in the document to make your Web page more attractive.

Lesson 5
Working with Graphics

In the Web development technology, the graphics can be defined as a visual representation of information in the form of pictures, graphs, and images. The right selection of graphics in a Web page helps in communicating the intended message effectively to the viewers. After inserting a graphic, you can edit it in the Dreamweaver workspace by modifying its various properties, such as brightness and contrast. Dreamweaver also allows you to create rollover images and image maps. In this lesson, you will learn how to insert an image as an object or background, set image properties, create rollover image and image maps, and wrap text around an image.

Teach Yourself Adobe Dreamweaver CS6 – By Niranjan Jha – Published by Cromosys

Inserting an Image

The websites are full of images. Dreamweaver provides several ways to insert an image into an HTML document. You can insert an image simply by selecting the Image option from the Insert menu. In addition, you can use INSERT, FILES, and ASSETS panels to insert an image in a Web page. Dreamweaver also allows you to insert an image as an object as well as a background in an HTML page. When you insert an image into the HTML document, a reference to the image file is automatically generated in the HTML source code. You can save your image files in the Root folder of your website to keep a track of files for easy website management. This also helps in maintaining the accurate reference of the image file in the HTML source code. However, if the image file is not located in the Root folder of your website, Dreamweaver prompts you to copy the file into the Root folder. Whenever you add an image to the document, the Image Tag Accessibility Attributes dialog box appears, prompting you to enter an alternative text (alt). If the image fails to display on Web browser, then the alternative text is displayed in place of the image. So this lesson explains you to insert an image as an object, as well as a background.

Inserting an Image as an Object

Images make your Web page beautiful. If you want your website to be attractive, you need to insert right images in it. Let us perform the following steps carefully to insert an image as an object in a web page:

1. **Click** the place where you want to insert an image in Articles.html document. For now, you can click below the heading (below Health Benefits) of the page.

2. Select **Insert> Image** option from the Menu bar to open the Select Image Source dialog box. Then **browse** to the location of the image file from the Look in list box, and select the desired image from the Contents pane, and then click **OK**.

3. If the image file is not present in the Root folder (Dreamweaver CS6 folder), the Dreamweaver message box appears indicating the user to copy the image file into the Root folder. In this case, the Image Tag Accessibility Attributes dialog box appears.

4. Click the **Browse** icon in the Image Tag Accessibility Attributes dialog box to copy the image to the Root folder. It opens the Select File dialog box.

5. **Browse** to the Dreamweaver CS6 folder where you need to copy the image. Then type the name: **title_image** of the copied image in the File name text box, and click **OK**.

6. The name of the image appears in the Long description text box in the Image Tag Accessibility Attributes dialog box. After you **click** OK to close this dialog box, you will see that the title_image is inserted at the selected place in your Web page.

Inserting an Image as an Background

Now you are going to insert an image as a background of the Web page. Perform the following steps on your computer:

1. Open the Web page **People Welfare.html** that you have already created. Then click the **Page Properties** button from the <u>CSS PROPERTIES</u> inspector. It opens the Page Properties dialog box.

2. Click the **Browse** button to locate the image file. It opens the <u>Select Image Source</u> dialog box. Then **browse** to the location of the image file from the <u>Look in</u> list box and **select** the desired image from the <u>Content</u> pane.

3. **Click** the OK button in the Select Image Source dialog box. The Page Properties dialog box reappears with the location of the image in the <u>Background image</u> text box.

4. **Click** OK button again to close the <u>Page Properties</u> dialog box. You will see that the image is inserted as a background in the Web page.

Setting Image Properties

You can use the PROPERTIES inspector to set the properties of an image. This can be done by changing various attributes of the image, such as Width, Height, Crop, Sharpen, Brightness, and Contrast. The list below shows the options available in the PROPERTIES:

W and H: Defines the width and height of the image in pixel value. Dreamweaver automatically updates the W and H text boxes, whenever any change is made in the dimensions of the image.
Src: Specifies the path or location of the image.
ID: Assigns and ID to the selected object.
Alt: Replaces the image with the alternative text for the text-only browsers (browser that download images manually). In some browsers, this text appears when the mouse-pointer sets over the image.
Link: Specifies the hyperlink for the image.
Align: Specifies the alignment of the image on the Web page.
V Space: Adds space in pixels along the top and bottom sides of the image.
H Space: Adds space in pixels along the right and left side of the image.
Target: Specifies the frame or window in which the hyperlink loads. This option is only used when you set the hyperlink in the image.
Border: Defines the width of the image border in pixels. By default, border is not applied to the image.
Edit: Opens the selected image in the external image editor.
Edit image settings: Opens the Image Preview dialog box that lets you optimize the image.
Sharpen: Adjusts the sharpness of the image.
Crop: Trims the size of the image by removing the unwanted areas of the image.
Brightness and Contrast: Adjusts the settings related to the brightness and contrast of the image.
Resample: Resizes the image by changing the number of pixels in the image.
Reset Size: Resets the width and height values of the image to its original values.
Hotspot Tool: Draws hotspots, such as pointer, rectangle, circle, and polygon on a selected image.

Now you can easily set and change the properties of an image in a Web page. Perform the following steps to change the properties of an image:

1. **Open** the Articles.html Web page and **select** the image title_image that you have inserted below the heading.

2. **Type** the value in the <u>Border</u> text box to specify the thickness of border for an image. For now, you can type: **5** as the value.

3. **Click** anywhere in the Document window to set the image. The border of the desired thickness is applied to the title_image.

Creating a Rollover Image

A rollover image is an image that changes when the mouse-pointer moves over it. You need to use two images, the primary image and the secondary image, to create a rollover image. The images used in the rollover should be of the same size. However, if the size of the primary image is not similar to the size of the secondary image, Dreamweaver automatically resizes the secondary image so that it matches with the properties of the primary image. Perform the following steps to create a rollover image:

1. **Open** a new Web page and **save** it with the name Cromosys.html. Then **click** the place where you want to insert the image.

2. Select **Insert> Image Objects> Rollover Image** from the Menu bar. It opens the <u>Insert Rollover Image</u> dialog box.

3. Click the **Browse** button beside the <u>Original image</u> text box to set the original image for the rollover. The Original Image dialog box appears.

4. **Select** the image that you want to insert in the rollover from the <u>Contents</u> pane, and click **OK** button. The selected image file is added in the Original image text box.

5. Click the **Browse** button beside the <u>Rollover image</u> text box to insert the rollover image. Then **select** the image from the Content pane of Rollover Image, and click **OK** button. The Rollover Image dialog box closes and the selected image is added in the Rollover image text box in the <u>Insert Rollover Image</u> dialog box.

6. Click **OK** button in the Insert Rollover Image dialog box. The rollover image is added in the Web page. Then go to **File> Preview in Browser> IExplore** from the Menu bar. It opens the Dreamweaver message box.

7. Click **Yes** in the Dreamweaver message box to save the changes. Then it opens the Cromosys.html Web page in Internet Explorer. If you place the mouse-pointer on the original image, it will display the rollover image.

Creating an Image Map

An image map is an image that is divided into regions known as hotspots. Every hotspot in an image map defines a behavior or action assigned to it. For example, when a user clicks a hotspot, it opens a new Web page. An image map can have multiple hotspots as well as multiple behaviors assigned to a hotspot. In Dreamweaver, you can create hotspots in various shapes, such as rectangle, polygon, and circle. A pointer hotspot is also available in Dreamweaver, which can be used to adjust the border of the hotspot. Perform the following steps in Articles.html Web page to create image maps:

1. **Select** the image on which you want to set the image map. For now, you can select title_image that you have already inserted in the Articles.html Web page. The **PROPERTIES** inspector displays the properties of the selected image.

2. **Type** the name of the image map in the Map text box which is at the bottom left corner in the PROPERTIES inspector. For now, you can type: **title_image** as the name of the image map.

3. Click the **Rectangle Hotspot Tool** button in the PROPERTIES inspector which appears just below the Map text box. Then **drag** the Rectangle Hotspot Tool on the image to create a rectangular hotspot. The Dreamweaver message box appears indicating the user to describe the image map in the Alt list box of the PROPERTIES inspector.

4. Click the **OK** button to close the message box. The hotspot is defined on the image. The various options related to the hotspot appear in the PROPERTIES inspector.

5. Click the **Browse for File** button (which is at the right side of the Link option) in the PROPERTIES inspector to specify a link file for the image map. It opens the **Select File** dialog box.

6. **Browse** to the location of the HTML file that you want to link from the Look in list box. In this case, **open** Dreamweaver CS6 folder, and **select** Cromosys.html file, and then **click** OK in the Select File dialog box. The selected HTML filename is added to the Link text box in the PROPERTIES inspector.

7. Go to **File> Preview in Browser> IExplore** from the Menu bar to preview the Web page. It opens the Dreamweaver message box.

8. Click **Yes** in the message box to save the changes. The **Articles.html** Web page opens in the Internet Explorer.

9. Click the **hotspot** in the image map, which will open the **Cromosys.html** linked Web page in the Internet Explorer. You can close the window after viewing the page.

Wrapping Text around an Image

Dreamweaver allows you to give your Web page a professional look by using the Align option present in the PROPERTIES inspector. Using the Align option, you can wrap the text around the image in various positions by using different options, such as Top, Middle, Bottom, Right, or Left. You can perform the following steps to wrap the text around the image:

1. **Select** the image title_image in Articles.html document. Then **click** down arrow of the Align option in the PROPERTIES inspector to wrap the text.

2. Select **Right** position from the dropdown list. You will see that the image is aligned to the right position in the document.

After working with images, let's now learn to work with hyperlinks in Dreamweaver. The next lesson will teach you the process of creating hyperlinks.

Rounding Border Corners
border-top-right-radius:*xx*px;   this will round the upper right corne
border-top-left-radius:*xx*px;
border-bottom-right-radius:*xx*px;
border-bottom-left-radius:*xx*px;

Lesson 6
Working with Hyperlinks

A hyperlink is a segment of text or a graphical item that links different Web pages or different locations of the same Web page. The region from which a hyperlink can be activated is called an anchor, and the destination page of the hyperlink is known as a target. In this lesson, you will learn to create different types of hyperlinks, edit a hyperlink, and delete a hyperlink.

Creating Different Types of Hyperlinks

In Dreamweaver, you can create text, graphics, email, and anchored hyperlinks. Suppose you wan to create a text hyperlink; in such case, you should select the required text and create a hyperlink using the PROPERTIES inspector. After creating the hyperlink, the selected text is highlighted. When you place a mouse pointer on the highlighted text, it displays the Hand tool that directs to the file referenced by the hyperlink. Now you are going to learn about creating a text hyperlink, image hyperlink, email hyperlink, and a named anchor hyperlink.

Creating a Text Hyperlink

A text hyperlink is extensively used by the users while viewing a website. You can perform the following steps to create a text hyperlink:

1. **Select** the text that you want to set as a hyperlink. For now, in Articles.html Web page, select the text **daily routine** which is in the fourth line in the document (already shown in picture 2.7).

2. Select **Insert> Hyperlink** from the Menu bar to open the Hyperlink dialog box. Then **click** Browse button to open the Select File dialog box.

3. **Browse** to the location of the HTML file that you want to set as a hyperlink from the Look in list box. In this case, **select** the file Cromosys.html from the Contents pane, and click **OK** in the Select File dialog box. The name of the linked html file, Cromosys.html appears in the Link combo box.

4. **Click** the OK button again to close the Hyperlink dialog box. Then select **File> Save** to save the changes.

5. Select **File> Preview in Browser> IExplore** from the Menu bar. The Articles.html Web page is opened in the Internet Explorer window. Then **click** the hyperlink (the text: daily routine) in the Web page. It will open the linked Web page, Cromosys.html in the Internet Explorer. You can close the websites window after viewing.

Creating an Image Hyperlink

Dreamweaver allows you to create an image hyperlink. In Web development technology, an image hyperlink is described as an image that directs the user to a new Web page or a different location within the same Web page. When you create a link to an image, the borders around the image are highlighted. You can use the PROPERTIES inspector to create an image link. Perform the following steps to create an image hyperlink:

Teach Yourself Adobe Dreamweaver CS6 – By Niranjan Jha – Published by Cromosys

1. **Select** the image in a Web page to create the image link. For now, you can select original_image from the Cromosys.html Web page.

2. Click the **Browse for File** button located beside the Link text box from the PROPERTIES inspector. It opens the Select File dialog box.

3. **Select** the required file from the Select File dialog box. For now, you can select **People Welfare** file. Then **click** the OK button from the Select File dialog box. The name of the linked file appears in the Link text box.

4. Select **File> Save** to save the changes. Then go to **File> Preview in Browser> IExplore** from the Menu bar. The Cromosys.html Web page is opened in Internet Explorer.

5. **Click** the image hyperlink in the Web page. The linked Web page, People Welfare.html is opened in Internet Explorer. You can close the websites at the end.

Creating an Email Hyperlink

Email hyperlinks are the hyperlinks that open a new message window of the default email application. These hyperlinks are used in case users want to provide feedback for the websites. In our case, we have added the following text on the People Welfare.html Web page:
Drop us your valuable feedback at: cromosys@yahoo.com
Perform the following steps to create an email hyperlink:

1. **Select** the text on which you want to set a hyperlink. In our case, we have selected the **cromosys@yahoo.com** text.

2. Select **Insert> Email Link** from the Menu bar. It opens the Email Link dialog box. The email address is automatically added in the Text and Email text boxes. However, if you want a different text or email address, you can specify it in the dialog box.

3. Click the **OK** button in the Email Link dialog box. Then select **File> Save** from the Menu bar to save the changes.

4. Go to **File> Preview in Browser> IExplore** to preview the Web page in Internet Explorer. Then **click** the **cromosys@yahoo.com** email link. It opens the Internet Explorer Security message box on the screen.

5. Click the **Allow** button in the message box. The new email message window of Microsoft Outlook is opened on the screen.

Creating Named Anchor Hyperlink

Named anchor hyperlink is a hyperlink that allows you to navigate between different locations within the same Web page or to a specific section of another Web page within the same website. You can find the named anchor hyperlinks mostly on Wikipedia webpage. Perform the following steps to create a named anchor hyperlink:

1. **Create** a new Web page named **Water.html**, and **type** some text about water in the page. Then **place** the cursor where you want to insert an anchor icon. For now, you can place the cursor at the end of the Water.html Web page.

2. Select **Insert> Named Anchor** from the Menu bar to open the Named Anchor dialog box. Then **type** the name of the anchor in the Anchor name text box as: **page_start**, and click **OK**. You will see that the anchor icon appears in the Water.html web page.

3. **Select** the text on which you want to set the named anchor. In this case, you can select the very first word (for example: ABC) of the text.

4. Now you need to type the name of the named anchor in the Link text box in the PROPERTIES inspector. For this, you can type: **# page_start** in the text box.

5. Select **File> Save** to save the changes. Then go to **File> Preview in Browser> IExplore** to preview the Web page in Internet Explorer. The Internet Explorer displays the Water.html Web page.

6. **Click** the named anchor text (for example: ABC). The named anchor automatically locates to the place where you have set the anchor icon. When you click on the named anchor hyperlink (ABC), you will see that the focus moves to the end of the Web page. You can close the websites at the end.

Editing a Hyperlink
In Dreamweaver, you can edit all types of hyperlinks using the Change Link option in the Modify menu or through the PROPERTIES inspector. Perform the following steps to edit a link using the Modify menu:

1. **Select** the hyperlink that you want to edit. Then go to **Modify> Change Link** from the Menu bar. It opens the Select File dialog box.

2. **Select** a different **.html** file from the Select File dialog box and click **OK** button. Then go to **File> Save** from the Menu bar to save the changes.

3. Choose **File> Preview in Browser> IExplore** to preview the Web page in Internet Explorer. The Internet Explorer displays the .html Web page.

4. **Click** the text hyperlink that you edited now. It opens the changed HTML file linked to the text hyperlink. You can close the websites at the end.

Deleting a Hyperlink
You can delete the link, which is no longer in use, by using the Remove Link option in the Modify menu. Perform the following steps to delete a hyperlink:

1. **Select** the hyperlink which is no longer in use in a Web page. You are going to delete the hyperlink permanently.

2. Choose **Modify> Remove Link** from the Menu bar of the Dreamweaver screen. The required hyperlink is deleted.

Lesson 7
Working with Multimedia

Websites are incomplete without audio and video elements. Majority of Web pages that we see on Internet today use a combination of video and sound files to gain popularity in terms of viewership and interactivity. You can also create similar Web pages by inserting video and sound files in your Web pages. The video or sound file starts playing when you click the play button of the video or audio element. In addition, you can edit the video or sound file as per your requirement. For example, if you observe that a Web page is taking too long to display a video file on a low bandwidth Internet connection, then you can simply trim the video file to decrease its size (measured in KB or MB) for faster display. In this lesson, you will learn about various formats of Flash files. You will also learn to insert an swf file, a video file, and a sound file in a Web page.

Understanding Flash File Formats

Dreamweaver allows you to add Flash content, such as movies and images, in your Web pages in various file formats, such as .fla, and .swf. Let us see about the file formats in detail:

The Flash file (.fla): Contains the source file of a Flash application. The .fla file opens only in Flash. It cannot be opened in Dreamweaver and Web browser. If you want to open this file in a Web browser, first open it in Flash and then export it to the Web browser as a .swf or .swt file. After exporting the file, the video element is visible in the Web browser, and you need to click the play button of the video element to play it.

The Flash swf file (.swf): Refers to the compressed version of the .fla file. The .swf file can be previewed in Dreamweaver and played in a Web browser. This file cannot be edited in Flash.

The Flash video file (.flv): Contains sound and video data in an encoded format.

The Flash template file (.swt): Enables you to modify and replace the information in a Flash .swf file format.

Inserting an SWF File

In Dreamweaver, you can insert an swf file and preview the same in the Design view of the Dreamweaver document. Dreamweaver allows you to set the properties for swf files using the PROPERTIES inspector. Perform the following steps on your computer to insert an swf file in the Web page:

1. **Open** the Web page in which you want to insert Flash file. Then **click** to place the cursor where the Flash content should be.

2. Choose **Insert> Media> SWF** to open the Select SWF dialog box. Then **select** the Flash file that you want to insert. In our case, we have selected **Action Play** file.

3. **Click** OK button at the bottom. It opens the Object Tag Accessibility Attributes dialog box, as shown in picture 2.8. This dialog box contains the following fields:

Title: Enters a title for the media object.

Access key: Enters a keyboard equivalent (one letter) to the object referred in the Title field. This letter can be pressed along with the Ctrl key to access the object.

Tab index: Enters a tab order number for the required object of the form.

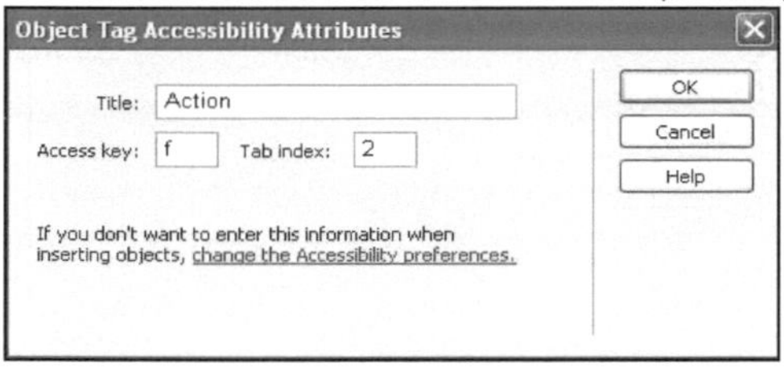

Picture 2.8

4. Type the title in the Title text box: **Action**, type the value for the access key in the Access key: **f**, and type the value for the tab index in the Tab index: **2**, as shown in picture 2.8.

5. **Click** the OK button on the dialog box. The Action Play file is inserted in the page. The page will look as shown in picture 2.9.

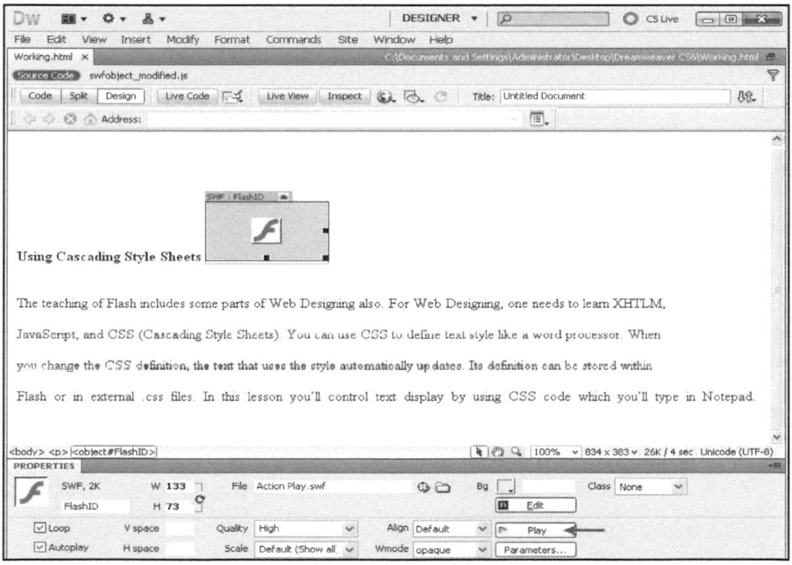

Picture 2.9

6. **Click** the Play button (shown with a red arrow in the picture 2.9) in the PROPERTIES inspector to play the Flash file. If you want to stop playing the file, you need to click the same button again in the PROPERTIES inspector.

Now let us discuss about the various options that are visible right now in the PROPERTIES inspector (shown in picture 2.9). As you can see on your screen also, these options appear after you insert a Flash file. The PROPERTIES inspector contains the following options:

W: Defines the width of the Flash content in pixels.
H: Defines the height of the Flash content in pixels.
File: Defines the path of the Flash content. You can click the folder icon to browse the file or type the path of the file in the File text box.
Src: Defines the path of the source file when both Dreamweaver and Flash are installed in a computer.
Bg: Defines the background color of the Flash content area. This color also appears while the Flash content is not playing.
Edit: Allows you to edit the Flash content.
Class: Defines the class name under which you want to place the Flash button.
Loop: Makes the Flash content to play repeatedly. If the Loop checkbox is not selected, the movie stops after playing once.
Autoplay: Enables Flash content to play automatically when the page loads.
V space: Defines the number of pixels of white spaces on right and left sides of the Flash content.
H space: Defines the number of pixels of white spaces on above and below portions of the Flash content.
Quality: Controls the anti-aliasing of the Flash content. A Flash content looks better with the High option setting, but it requires a faster processor to render correctly on the screen.
Scale: Defines how the Flash content fits into the dimensions set in the width and height of the area defined for the Flash content.
Align: Defines how the Flash content can be aligned on the Web page.
Wmode: Sets the Wmode parameter for the swf file to avoid conflicts with the DHTML elements, such as Spray widgets.
Play: Displays the preview of the Flash content in the Design view of the Document window.
Parameters: Opens the Parameters dialog box. You can add parameters to the Flash content in the Parameters dialog box.

Inserting a Video File
In the early days, it was difficult for Web designers and developers to use video on the Internet. They had to contend with low-bandwidth connections that made downloading of data-intensive video files impossible. In addition, users had to install special players to view video in pop-up windows. However, things have been changed since then. Web designers and developers are using Flash video format to ensure that visitors can view a video without downloading additional plug-ins. In this section, you will learn to insert a Flash video file, and a video from YouTube.

Inserting a Flash Video File
Dreamweaver allows you to insert Flash files in Web pages. These Flash files have .flv extension and can be inserted in the Web page using the Insert menu. However, to play these files, you must have the Flash player installed on your system. If the Flash player is not installed, the Web browser window will display the instructions for downloading it. Perform the following simple steps to insert a Flash video file in a Web page:

1. **Open** the desired Web page, and **select** the element where you want to insert the Flash video file. The element can be anything such as a rectangular box, as shown in picture 3.0 with a red arrow.

Picture 3.0

2. Choose **Insert> Media> FLV** from the Menu bar. It opens the Insert FLV dialog box which you can see in the picture 3.1.

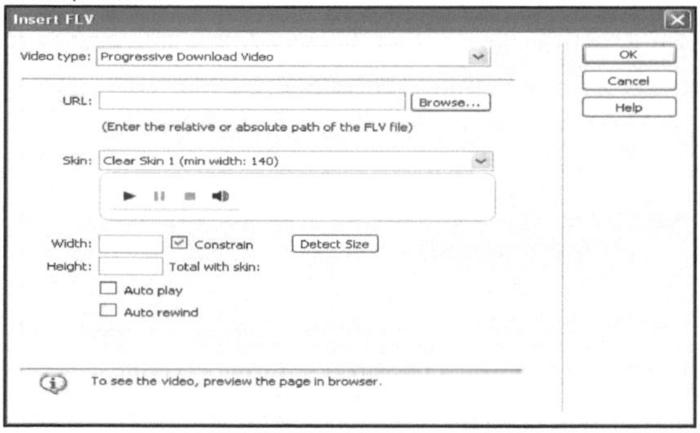

Picture 3.1

When you look at the Insert FLV dialog box on your screen, you will see that this dialog box contains various options. Here is the description of those options:

Video type: Offers Flash video type to the website visitors. The video types are as follows:
- **Progressive Download Video option:** Downloads the Flash video file to the website visitors' hard disk and then plays it.
- **Streaming Video option:** Streams the Flash video file and plays it on a Web page after a short buffer period that ensures smooth playback.

URL: Defines the relative or absolute path to the Flash video file.

Teach Yourself Adobe Dreamweaver CS6 – By Niranjan Jha – Published by Cromosys

Skin: Defines the appearance of the Flash video component. The preview of the selected skin appears under the Skin pop-up menu.

Width: Defines the width of the section on the Web page where the Flash video file is displayed, in pixels.

Height: Specifies the height of the section on the Web page where the Flash video file is displayed, in pixels.

Constrain: Maintains the aspect ratio between the width and height of the selected skin. This check box is selected by default.

Detect Size: Displays the default height and width for the Flash video file.

Auto play: Specifies whether to play the Flash video file while opening the Web page.

Auto rewind: Defines whether the playback control returns to the start position after the video finishes playing.

3. Click the **Browse** button which opens the Select FLV dialog box. **Locate** the Flash video file saved in your hard drive, and click **OK**. The URL of the selected Flash video file appears in the URL text box in the Insert FLV dialog box.

4. Click the **Detect Size** button to automatically set the height and width of the inserted Flash video file. The height and width values appear in their respective text boxes. Then click **OK** button to make the video file appear in the Web page.

5. Choose **File> Save** from the Menu bar to save the changes. Then select **File> Preview in Browser> IExplore** to view the Web page in Internet Explorer. The Web page opens in Internet Explorer.

6. Click the **Play** button now. It will play the Flash video file on the screen. In the next section, you will learn to insert a video file from YouTube.

Inserting a Video from YouTube

Dreamweaver also allows you to insert videos in your Web pages directly from a website that has some preloaded videos. Usually, such videos are uploaded on a website by its users free of cost for general public. You can insert these freely available videos in your Web pages. One such site, which can be useful to obtain free videos, is YouTube. Through YouTube, you can browse variety of videos and insert them in your Web page. Perform the following simple steps to insert a Video from YouTube:

1. **Go to** the YouTube website, and **open** the video that you want to insert in your Web page. Then **click** the Embed button on YouTube which is just below the video. It opens the code of the video.

2. **Copy** the code by dragging the mouse-pointer over it. Then **open** your Web page in the Coder view and **click** at the desired place to insert the video.

3. **Paste** the code of the video, and click the **Refresh** button at the top. The code as well as the Refresh button is shown in the picture 3.2 with a red arrow. On your screen, you may find the Refresh button also at the right side in the middle of the Panel Group, under CSS STYLES section.

4. Choose **File> Save** from the Menu bar to save the changes. Then select **File> Preview in Browser> IExplore** to view the Web page in Internet Explorer. The Web page opens in Internet Explorer.

Picture 3.2

5. Click the **Play** button to play the video. In the next section, you will learn to insert a sound file on the Web page.

Inserting Sound

Sound makes the Web pages more expressive. For instance, if you are creating an online tutorial, you can add sound files in your Web pages. Dreamweaver allows you to import these sounds. Various sound formats supported by Dreamweaver are Musical Instrument Digital Interface (.midi or .mid), Waveform Extension (.wav), Audio Interchange File Format or AIFF (.aif), or Motion Picture Experts Group Audio or MPEG-Audio Layer-3 (.mp3). Perform the following steps to insert sound in a Web page:

1. **Open** the Web page and **click** at the desired place to insert the sound. Then select **Insert> Media> Plugin** from the Menu bar. It opens the Select File dialog box.

2. **Select** the required sound file, and click the **OK** button. The sound file is inserted in the Web page. You can **drag** to set the size of the sound file in the Web page.

3. Choose **File> Save** to save the changes. Then select **File> Preview In Browser> IExplore** to preview the Web page in Internet Explorer. The Web page opens in Internet Explorer.

4. Click the **play** button in the sound section to play the sound file. The inserted sound starts playing in the Web page.

Lesson 8
Working with HTML Objects

You can present information with the help of tables, framesets, and frames. A table is a collection of rows and columns that can be used to display bulk data, such as a telephone list or an address list. A frameset is a Web document that contains frames and information related to each frame, such as size, position on Web page, and links to target frames. Using frames, you can display multiple Web pages in a single Web browser. Consider a Web page, which is divided into two frames. One frame can consist of a menu of hyperlinks and another frame can display the content for each menu item. When a user clicks a hyperlink, the related content is then opened in another frame. The concept behind a frame is very simple; instead of using a single Web page to display the information or content, you can divide the Web page into multiple frames, each of which displays a separate Web page. This approach of displaying content in multiple frames enhances the user-friendliness of the websites you create. While tables, framesets, and frames are used to represent information on a Web page, HTML forms are used to receive information, such as feedback or personal details, from the visitors of a website. An HTML form may contain text fields, buttons, check boxes, radio buttons, dropdown lists, and menus.

Working with Tables

A table is a collection of data arranged in rows and columns. In other words, a table helps you to display information in an easy to read and understand format of rows and columns. The intersection of a row and column creates cells, where you can enter your text, image, or other controls such as buttons. You can also increase the number of rows and columns in a table or add more than one table in the Web page. Dreamweaver allows you to create a table in the Code view or the Design view. You can modify the table by merging and splitting cells, change the fill color of cells, rows, or columns, and set table properties by using the PROPERTIES inspector. The information in the table can also be sorted in ascending and descending order. In addition, Dreamweaver allows you to import information in a table from other applications. In the following sections, you are going to learn to create a table, edit a table, sort a table, and import data into a table.

Creating Tables and Inserting Text

In the past, tables were designed manually by using the HTML code. With the help of Dreamweaver, you can easily create tables in the Design view by simply entering a few values to specify the number of rows and columns for the table. In addition, Dreamweaver allows you to add a table in a cell of another table by using the same procedure of creating a table. Perform the following steps to create a table in a Web page:

1. **Create** a new Web page or open a desired Web page in Dreamweaver. Then **place** the cursor where you want to insert the table.

2. Choose **Insert> Table** from the Menu bar to open the Table dialog box (shown in picture 3.3). This dialog box contains the following options to set the table properties:

Rows: Determines the number of rows in the table.
Columns: Determines the number of columns in the table.
Table width: Specifies the width of the table in pixels or as a percentage of the browser window's width.
Border thickness: Specifies the width of the table's border in pixels.

Cell spacing: Allows you to set the spacing between text, numbers, or alphanumeric characters typed in a cell. For example, you can set distance of 5 pixels between each character typed in a cell.

Cell padding: Allows you to set empty space between cell border and information appearing in a cell. You can set spacing from top, bottom, left, or right border of a cell. For example, you can set spacing of 10 pixels from left border of a cell so that text appears a little bit away from the border.

None: Disables column or row headings for the table.

Left: Makes the first column (that is, the left side) of the table as the heading.

Top: Makes the first row of the table as the heading.

Both: Allows you to type headings for rows and columns.

Caption: Provides a title for the table, which is displayed outside the table.

Summary: Provides the description of the table.

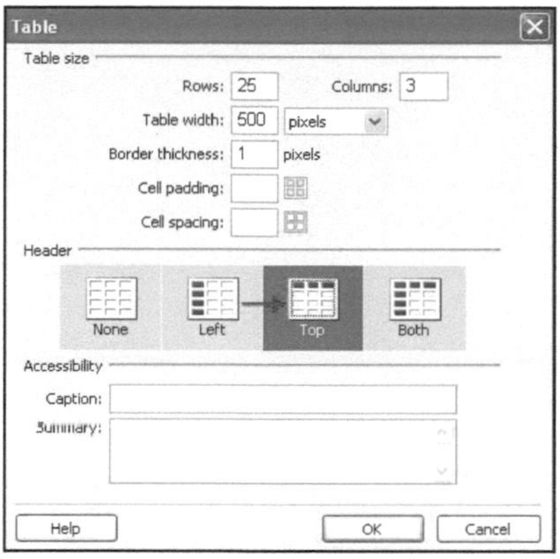

Picture 3.3

3. **Specify** the number of rows as: **25**, number of columns as: **3**, and table width as: **500** pixels. These specifications are also shown in picture 3.3.

4. In the Header section, select the **Top** option as the table header, as shown in the picture with a red arrow.

5. **Click** the OK button in the Table dialog box. The table is inserted in the Web page.

Dreamweaver also allows you to add text, graphics, multimedia files, and other content inside table cells. You can perform the following simple steps on your Dreamweaver screen to insert the text into the table that you have created.

6. **Select** the cell (any one) where you want to insert the data. Then **type** the required text, such as: **Name**. Similarly, you can type the text in the other cells of the table.

Editing Tables

After creating a table, you can modify it by merging and splitting cells, formatting the cells, or setting the table properties. You can perform all these modifications by using the PROPERTIES inspector. In case you do not require a particular table, you can easily remove it by selecting the specific table and pressing the Delete key from the keyboard. So in this section, you will learn to merge cells in a table, and set table properties.

Merging Cells in a Table

Merging table cells refers to combining two or more cells into one. And splitting table cells means breaking a cell into two or more rows or columns. You can customize a table structure by merging and splitting the rows or columns. You can merge and split a cell by using either the Table submenu under the Modify menu or the PROPERTIES inspector. Perform these steps to merge cells into a single cell:

1. **Select** <u>all the three</u> cells of the first row in the Web page. You need to drag the mouse-pointer over them.

2. **Click** the <u>Merges selected cells using spans</u> button from the PROPERTIES inspector. This option is at the bottom left side (below Row option) in the PROPERTIES inspector. The selected cells are merged and appear as a single cell.

Setting Table Properties

Dreamweaver allows you to set various properties of a table, such as text alignment, font style, or color scheme. You can use the PROPERTIES inspector to set different properties of the table. However, it is not mandatory to specify a value for each property. Instead, you can set the values of only those properties that best fulfill your requirements. Whenever a table cell is selected, all the related properties are enabled in the PROPERTIES inspector, as shown in picture 3.4.

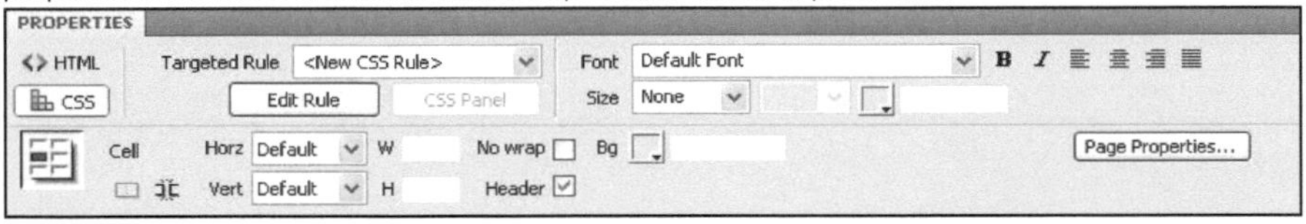

Picture 3.4

Now let us discuss about these table cell properties of the PROPERTIES inspector. We will start with the options available on the left side.

Horz: Specifies the horizontal alignment of the content in a cell, row, or column. You can align the content to the left, right, or center of the cell, or use the browser's default alignment (which is usually left for regular cells and center for header cells).

Vert: Specifies the vertical alignment of the content in a cell, row, or column. You can align the content to the top, middle, bottom, or baseline of the cells, or use the browser's default alignment.

W: Specifies the width of the selected cells in pixels or as a percentage of the entire table's width. You can specifies the percentage by adding the percent symbol (%) after the value of the table width. If you want the browser to determine the proper width based on the content of the cell and the width of the other columns and rows, leave this field blank (default).

H: Specifies the height of the selected cells in pixels or as a percentage of the entire table's height. You can either specify the percentage by using the percent symbol after the height value or leave the field blank to enable the browser to set the height based on the content of the cell.

Bg (lower color swatch and text field): Sets the background color of a cell, column, or row selected with the help of the color picker.

Bg (text box): Displays hexadecimal value of selected background color of a table cell, column, or row.

Merge Cells: Combines the selected table cells, rows, or columns into one cell.

Split Cell: Divides a cell into two or more cells. You can split only one cell at a time; this property is disabled if more than one cell is selected.

No wrap: Prevents automatic adjustment (wrapping) of text according to the width of the cell. If the No wrap property is enabled, the cells expand automatically to accommodate the text as it is typed or pasted into a cell.

Header: Formats the selected cell as a table header cell. The content of the table header cell is bold and centered by default.

After leaning about the table cell properties of the PROPERTIES inspector, perform the following steps to set the background color of the cell in the table:

1. **Select** the first row (three cells) of the table to change the background color. Then **click** down arrow button of the **Bg** option in the PROPERTIES inspector. It will open the color palette.

2. **Choose** a color using the color picker. The color you choose is represented by the **#FFCCCC** code. The selected color is applied to the row. By the way, you can also type the value of a color in the text box beside the Bg option.

Sorting Table Data

Sorting refers to the process of sequentially arrange data or information of a table. A table can be sorted in two ways, in ascending order or in descending order. You can either sort the rows of a table based on the content of one or more columns or sort table data by suing the Sort Table option available in the Commands menu. The Sort Table option displays the Sort Table dialog box from where you can specify and set the necessary properties to sort the data of the table. However, you can set these properties only when the table does not contain rowspan or calspan. The following are the options available in the Sort Table dialog box:

Sort by: Determines the column according to which the rows of a table are sorted.
Order: Determines the alphabetical or numerical order to sort a table column. In addition, you can also set the sequence to sort the data of the table, either as ascending (A to Z, lower numbers to higher numbers) or as descending (Z to A, higher numbers to lower numbers).
Then by/Order: Determines the sorting order for a secondary sort on a different column.
Sort includes the first row: Specifies whether to include the first row of the table in the sort.
Sort header rows: Sorts all table rows in the header section.
Sort footer rows: Sorts all table rows in the footer section.
Keep all row colors the same after the sort has been completed: Specifies that table row attributes (such as color) should remain associated with the same content after the sort.

After knowing about the options available in the Sort Table, you can easily sort the data of a table. To get the practical knowledge of this, perform the following steps on your computer to sort the data of a table:

1. **Select** the required table or click any cell of the table that you want to sort. Then choose **Command>Sort Table** from the Menu bar to open the Sort Table dialog box.

2. From the Order dropdown list, select **Alphabetically** and **Descending**. Then click **OK** button in the Sort table dialog box. You will see that the data in the table in sorted in the descending order with respect to the first column.

Importing Data in a Table

If you import financial data or other spreadsheet information manually in Dreamweaver, it can be a very tedious job. For this reason, Dreamweaver allows you to insert tabular data created in other applications, such as Microsoft Word or Excel, in the currently opened Web page. However, before you import or insert data from other applications, you must save the data in a specified format and separate it by using the required elements such as tabs, commas, colons, or semicolons. For example, many spreadsheet applications, such as Microsoft Excel, allow you to save data in a specific format known as Comma Separated Values (CSV). After saving the data in the specified format, you can easily import the data into Dreamweaver. Perform the following steps to import data into a table:

1. **Create** a new Web page or open an existing Web page to import information from another application. Then select **File> Import> Tabular Data** from the Menu bar. It opens the Import Tabular Data dialog box.

2. Click the **Browse** button in the Import Tabular Data dialog box. Then in the Open dialog box, **select** the required file and click **Open** at the bottom. The path of the selected file is added to the Data file text box of the Import Tabular Data dialog box.

3. Click **OK** button in the Import Tabular Data dialog box. You will see on your screen that the imported file is inserted into the Web page.

see pg 42

Lesson 9

Working with Framesets and Frames no longer available - use Division

Using frames, you can split a Web page into segments, with each frame displaying a different HTML file. A frame displays an HTML file independent of the other frames in the Web page. For instance, if a Web page has two frames, it can display two HMTL pages.

A frameset defines the framing structure of an HTML file that includes the arrangement of frames, the size of the frames, and the attributes shared among the frames. A frameset is a collection of frames and it can never be displayed by itself. Frames, on the other hand, are complete HTML files that can be viewed and edited separately, or in the format described by the frameset. Let's now learn to create and save a frameset and a frame.

Creating Framesets and Frames

Dreamweaver allows you to present your HTML file in multiple views by using frames. You need to create the HTML file in the structure of a frameset to use frames in a Web page. When you create a frameset, remember that each frame area is a separate HTML file. Here are the steps to create a frameset with frames:

1. Choose **File> New** from the Menu bar of the Dreamweaver screen. It opens the New Document dialog box, as shown in picture 3.5.

2. Select the **Page from Sample** option which is on the left side of the New Document dialog box. Then select the **Frameset** option in the Sample Folder section. And then, select **Fixed Top, Fixed Bottom** frameset from the Sample Page section.

3. Click the **Create** button at the bottom. It opens the Frame Tag Accessibility Attributes dialog box on the screen.

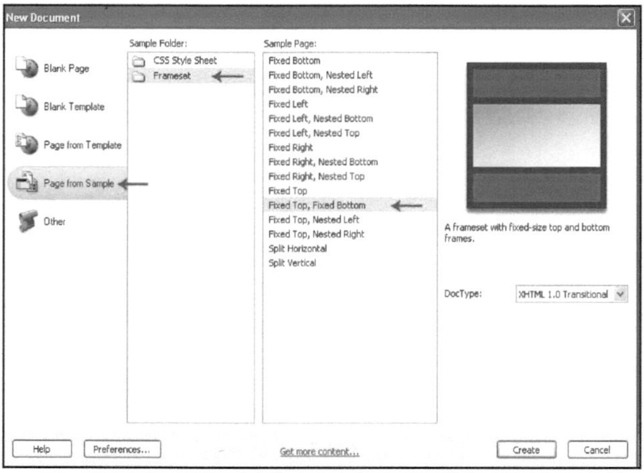

Picture 3.5

4. Select the required option from the Frame dropdown list to set the title of each frame in the selected frameset. For now, you can select the **topFrame** option.

5. **Type** the desired title (for example: 1st frame) of the selected frame in the Title text box. Similarly you can **specify** the name of other two layers, as **2nd frame** and **3rd frame**.

6. Click the **OK** button on the Frame Tag Accessibility Attributes dialog box.

After you click the OK button on the Frame Tag Accessibility Attributes dialog box, a new frameset with a set of three frames is inserted in the Document, as shown in picture 3.6.

Picture 3.6

Saving a Frameset and Frame

You need to save a frameset in Dreamweaver to preview the frameset in Internet Explorer. Each frame in a frameset is considered as a separate HTML page. Therefore, you need to save each frame of the frameset as a separate file in Dreamweaver. Perform the following steps to save a frameset and a frame:

Teach Yourself Adobe Dreamweaver CS6 – By Niranjan Jha – Published by Cromosys

1. Choose **File> Save Frameset As** from the Menu bar. It opens the <u>Save As</u> dialog box. Then **browse** to the location from the <u>Save in</u> list box where you want to save the frameset.

2. **Type** the name of the frameset (for example: First_ frameset), and click the **Save** button at the bottom of the Save As dialog box. The frameset is saved with the name, and the name appears in the title bar of the Dreamweaver workspace.

As you can see in the picture 3.6 above, there are three frames inserted in the document with their names as 1st frame, 2nd frame, and 3rd frame. So you need to save these <u>frames</u> in a frameset now.

3. Click to select the **1st frame** which is the top frame in the document. When you click the first frame, the cursor starts blinking at the top left corner of the frame indicating that it is selected. Then choose **File> Save Frame** to open the <u>Save As</u> dialog box.

4. **Browse** to the location <u>Dreamweaver CS6 folder</u> from the Save in list box. Then **type** the name of the frame as: **Frame1_frameset**, and click the **Save** button.

The frame is saved with the specified name. When you click the frame in the Web page, the name of the frame appears in the title bar of the Dreamweaver workspace. Similarly, you can save the other frames in the frameset.

Exploring Frameset and Frame Properties
The properties of a frameset or frame appear in the PROPERTIES inspector when you select the FRAMES panel from the Windows menu. The settings in the PROPERTIES inspector control the appearance of the different viewable parts of a frame or frameset. You can use the PROPERTIES inspector to set properties, such as borders, margins, or scroll bar in a frame. The following options are enabled in the PROPERTIES inspector when you select a frameset from the FRAMES panel:

Borders: Displays the border around frames when the Web page is viewed in Internet Explorer. To prevent Internet Explorer from displaying borders, select No. you can select the Default option to allow Internet Explorer to determine how borders are displayed.
Border width: Specifies the width for all the borders in the frameset.
Border color: Sets the color for the borders. You can use the color picker to select the color or type the hexadecimal value for the color.
RowCol selection: Sets the size for the rows and columns for the frameset in the document. You can select the tab on the left side or top of the Row Col Selection area and enter the height value or width value in the Value text box.
Units: Specifies the unit of space that Internet Explorer allocates to each frame. Unit options include Pixels, Percent, and Relative.

The following options are enabled in the PROPERTIES inspector when you select a frame from the FRAMES panel:

Frame name: Specifies the name of the frame. A frame name should be a single word. The hyphens (-), periods (.), and spaces are not allowed in a name. In addition, a frame name must start with a letter and not a numeral. Note that the name of a frame is case-sensitive.

Src: Specifies the source file that is displayed in the frame. You need to click the folder icon to browse and select the source file.

Scroll: Specifies whether scroll bars appear in the frame or not. The Scroll dropdown list contains options that include Yes, No, Default, and Auto. Setting the option to Default allows each browser to use its default value. On the other hand, setting this option to Auto means that scroll bars will appear only when there is not enough space in a browser window to display the full content of the frame. If you set the Scroll property to No, then scroll bar will not appear in the frame.

No resize: Prevents users from dragging the frame borders to resize the frame in a browser.

Borders: Shows or hides the borders of the frame in a browser. Border options include Yes, No, and Default.

Border color: Sets a border color for all the borders of the frame in the frameset. This color applies to all the borders that touch the frame, and overrides the border color specified for the frameset.

Margin width: Sets the width in pixels of the left and right margins of the frame.

Margin height: Sets the height in pixels of the top and bottom margins of the frame.

After exploring frameset and frame properties, in the next section of the lesson, you will learn to set the properties for the frameset, and set the properties for the frame. Let us start the section with setting frameset properties.

Setting Frameset Properties

When you click the border of a frame in the Dreamweaver workspace or on the FRAMES panel, the properties of the frameset related to the frame are displayed in the PROPERTIES inspector. The various properties you can set for the frameset include those related to the width and color of the frameset's border. Perform the following steps to set the properties of a frameset:

1. Choose **Window> Frames** from the Menu bar. It opens the FRAMES panel in the Dreamweaver workspace, as shown in picture 3.7.

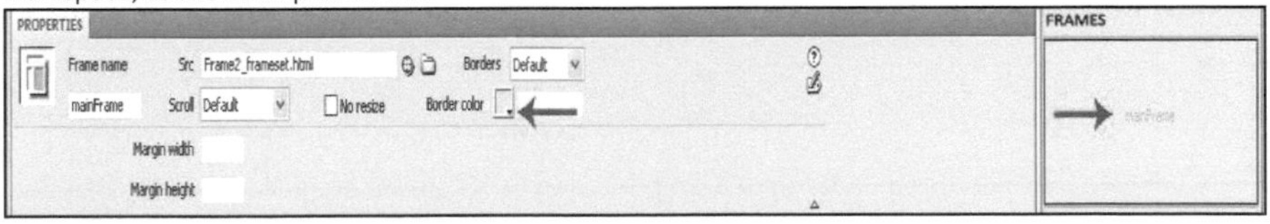

Picture 3.7

2. In the FRAMES panel, **select** the border of the frameset whose properties you want to set. Then in PROPERTIES inspector, **click** beside the Borders option and select **Yes** from the dropdown.

3. **Specify** the Border width as: **5** in the Border text box. Then **select** the Border color option by clicking the arrow beside the Border color, and select the **blue color** from the color palette. It will show the hexadecimal value of the blue color as #3300FF.

Now look at the border in the Dreamweaver workspace. You will see that the blue color is applied as the border color to the selected frameset. In the next section, you are going to learn about setting frame properties.

Setting Frame Properties

You can use the PROPERTIES inspector to set all the properties related to frames, such as size and color of the frame's border, or the options related to the scroll bar. Perform the following steps to set the properties of a frame:

1. **Select** the desired frame from the FRAMES panel, whose properties you want to set. For now, you can select the **mainframe**, as already shown in picture 3.7. The options related to the selected frame appear in the PROPERTIES inspector.

2. **Uncheck** the No resize check box from the PROPERTIES inspector. Then **drag** the mouse pointer in the Document window to resize the border of the selected frame. You need to drag the mouse pointer downward to decrease the height of the frame, as shown in picture 3.8. Resizing the frame changes the properties of the frame in the frameset and enables the frameset properties in the PROPERTIES inspector.

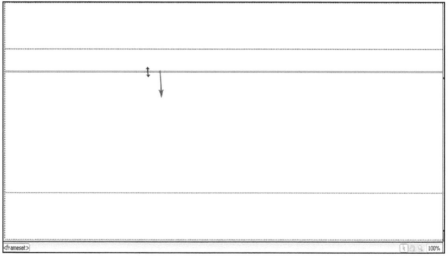

Picture 3.8

3. **Select** the frame named mainframe again to display the properties in the PROPERTIES inspector. Then **click** the Browse for file button to browse an HTML file that you want to open in the frame named mainframe. The select HTML File dialog box appears.

4. **Browse** to the Dreamweaver CS6 folder, and **select** the Articles.html file, and then click **OK** at the bottom. You will see on your screen that the Articles.html file opens in the frame named mainframe with the settings applied to the frame.

Similarly, you can apply the settings to all the frames of a frameset. Note that you need to save the changes before viewing the Web page in a browser. Now that you know how to set the properties of frames and framesets, let us learn about setting links to a target frame in the following section.

Setting Links to Target Frames

The frame in which a linked Web page appears is known as the target frame. The Target attribute of the Link option specifies the frame or window in which the linked content opens. The following are the options available in the target fame:

_blank: Opens the linked document in a new browser window.
_parent: Opens the linked document in the parent file of the Web page that contains the link.
_self: Opens the linked document. The opened document appears in the original frame and replaces the existing content of the frame.
_top: Opens the linked document in the window occupied by the current frameset; thereby, replacing the frameset completely.

Now let us do some practice on it. Perform the following steps on your computer to create a link to a target frame:

1. Create a new frameset or **open** an existing one named **First_ frameset** which you created in the previous section.

2. **Select** the image or any object that you want to set as a link. Then **click** the Browse for file button beside the Link text box in the PROPERTIES inspector. It opens the Select File dialog box.

3. **Select** the required HTML file that you want to open on clicking a hyperlink, and click the **OK** button. The hyperlink is set to the selected image.

4. **Click** the down arrow button of the Target combo box in the PROPERTIES inspector. Then you need to select the **–self** option from the dropdown list.

5. Choose **File> Save All** to save the changes. Then select **File> Preview in Browser> IExplore** to view the Web page in Internet Explorer. The Web page is opened in the browser window.

6. **Click** the hyperlink to open the linked page. You will see on your screen that the linked page also opens in the browser window.

Lesson 10
Working with HTML Forms

You have already learnt that HTML forms are used to collect information, such as feedback and personal details from the site visitors. These forms also allow you to perform various tasks, such as signing up for services, filling an online application, and sending your comments, queries, and suggestions. Dreamweaver helps in designing an HTML form by providing you several objects, such as radio button, check boxes, dropdown list, text field, text area, and buttons. In the next sections, you will learn to insert these objects in an HTML form.

Inserting a Text Field

The text field element is the most common element used while creating a form. Text field in a form allows you view the text in a proper manner that a user enters in a form. Perform the following steps to insert a text field in a Web page:

1. **Create** a new Web page in Dreamweaver, and **select** the place by inserting the cursor in the Web page where you want the text field.

2. Choose **Insert> Form> Text Field** from the Menu bar. It opens the Input Tag Accessibility Attributes dialog box.

3. Type: **textfield1** in the ID option text box, and click the **OK** button. It will become the ID of your text field. A message box appears to confirm the addition of the form tag.

4. **Click** the Yes button on the message box. The text field (beside the name text) appears in the Web page, as shown in the picture 3.9.

Picture 3.9

Inserting a Radio Button
Radio buttons are used when you want a user to select only one option out of the set of multiple options. For example, if you want to know the gender of a user, then you can create a gender option with two radio buttons: male and female, where the user can select the appropriate radio button. Perform the following steps to insert a radio button in a Web page:

1. **Select** the place in the Web page where you want to insert the radio button. Then choose **Insert> Form> Radio Button** from the Menu bar. It opens the Input Tag Accessibility Attributes dialog box.

2. Type: **radioButton1** in the ID option for your radio button. Then, **type** the text: **Male** in the Label text box which will appear as label with the radio button.

3. **Click** the OK button in the dialog box to insert the radio button. Similarly, you can create one more radio button for Female text, as shown in picture 4.0.

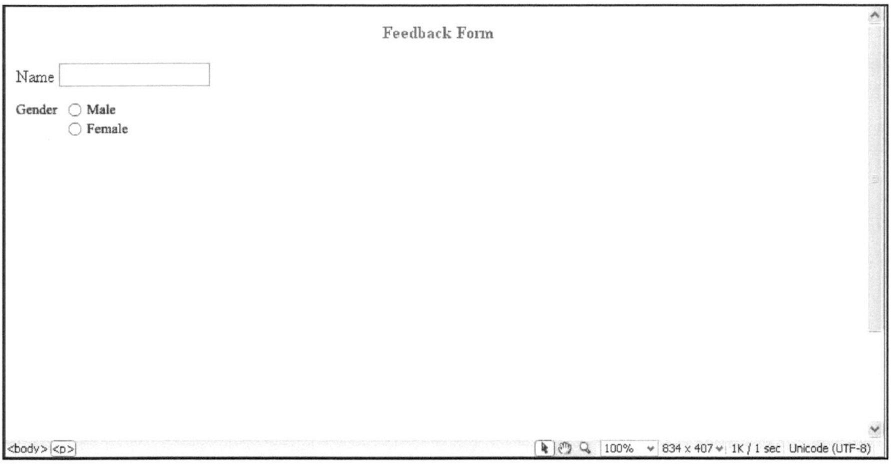

Feedback Form

Name

Gender ○ Male
○ Female

`<body> <p>`   100% 834 x 407 1K / 1 sec Unicode (UTF-8)

Picture 4.0

Inserting a Dropdown List

A dropdown list allows you to choose a value from a list of values. The dropdown list is read only, which implies that you cannot make any changes in it. Perform the following steps to insert a dropdown list in a Web page:

1. **Select** the place in the Web page where you want to insert the dropdown list. Then choose **Insert> Form> Select (List/Menu)** from the Menu bar.

2. Type: **listBox1** in the ID option for your dropdown list, and click the **OK** button in the dialog box. The dropdown list appears in the Web page.

3. Click the **List Values** button in the PROPERTIES inspector to add the list items. It opens the <u>List Values</u> dialog box.

4. **Type** values for the list items. In this case, you can type: **Student**, as the first list item. Then, you need to **click** the **Plus (+)** button to add the items. On the contrary, the Minus (-) button removes the items from the list.

5. You can **add** more list items depending on the requirement, such as Business man, Housewife, and Salaried employee.

6. **Click** the OK button in the end. You will see on your Dreamweaver screen that the specified items appear in the dropdown list, as shown in picture 4.1. In the next section, you will learn to insert a text area in a Web page.

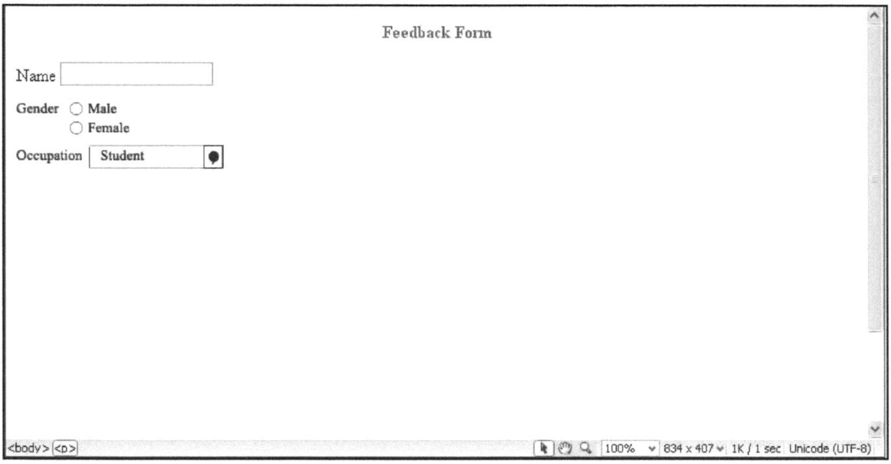

Picture 4.1

Inserting a Text Area
Using the text area element in a form, you can retrieve multiline data from the user. This is beneficial when you want the user to enter multiple lines of text, such as address or feedback. Perform the following steps to insert the text area in a Web page:

1. **Select** the place in the Web page where you want to insert the text area. Then choose **Insert> Form> Textarea** from the Menu bar.

2. Type: **textArea1** in the ID option for your text area, and click the **OK** button in the dialog box. The text area appears in the Web page. You will see the picture of it at the end of this lesson in picture 4.2.

Inserting a Check Box
Check boxes are used when you want users to select more than one option from the set of multiple options. Perform the following steps to insert a check box in an HTML form:

1. **Save** this Untitled Web page with the name **feedback.html**. Then **place** the cursor in the Web page where you want to insert the check box.

2. Choose **Insert> Form> Checkbox** from the Menu bar. Then, type: **checkbox1** in the ID option for your check box, and click the **OK** button in the dialog box. The check box appears in the Web page.

3. **Type** the required text that you want to insert after the check box. You can enter the text: **If the information provided by you is correct**. You will see the picture of it at the end of this lesson in picture 4.2.

Teach Yourself Adobe Dreamweaver CS6 – By Niranjan Jha – Published by Cromosys

Inserting a Button

The button element in a form can be used for different purposes. However, the most common use of a button is to submit or reset the information. While the Submit button enables user to submit the information entered in a form, the Reset button enables the user to clear the content of the form. Perform the following steps to insert a button:

1. **Place** the cursor in the Web page where you want to insert the button. Then choose **Insert> Form> Button** from the Menu bar.

2. Type: **button1** in the ID option for your text box, and click the **OK** button in the dialog box. The button with the default value Submit, is inserted in the Web page.

3. Select File> Save to save the changes made in the Web page. The feedback.html Web page is saved. Then select File> Preview in Browser> IExplore to preview the Web page in Internet Explorer, as shown in picture 4.2.

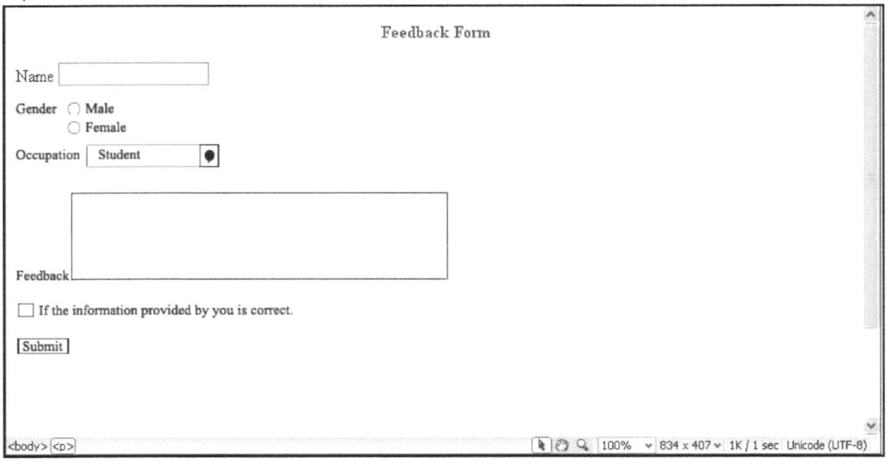

Picture 4.2

Lesson 11
Introducing Cascading Style Sheets

Cascading Style Sheets (CSS) is a collection of formatting rules, known as CSS rules, which controls the appearance of content in a Web page. CSS allows style information to be specified in various ways. Styles can be specified inside a single Hypertext Markup Language (HTML) element, inside the <head> element of an HTML page, or in an external CSS file. Even multiple external style sheets can be referenced inside a single HTML document. CSS positions elements within a Web page by using rectangular boxes, known as Absolute Positioned (AP) elements. These AP elements are used to hold and place the content of the Web page. When you create a Web page layout by using CSS, you will notice the use of <div> tags. The <div> tag creates areas or divisions within the Web page and places the content of the Web page in those areas. When you draw an AP element by using the Draw AP Div tool,

Dreamweaver inserts a <div> tag in the HTML code of the Web page. The AP element with the <div> tag is known as an AP Div element. In this lesson, you will learn about CSS, the CSS STYLES panel, and the CSS layout. You will also learn how to create new CSS rules and edit them. In addition, this lesson will discuss about the external CSS style sheets, and AP Div elements.

Defining Cascading Style Sheets

CSS defining rules reside either in an external CSS file or in the HTML code of the Web page, normally in the head section of the HTML code. Defining rules in the external CSS file makes it easy to maintain the appearance of all the Web pages associated with it. Consequently, you do not need to update the properties of every page whenever you make a change in a Web page. Instead, you only need to change the respective properties in the external CSS file, and the changes are automatically applied to all the linked Web pages. CSS offers you great flexibility and control over the appearance of your Web page. Using CSS, you can control the properties of a Web page, such as fonts, text color, background color, images, and tables.

CSS Rules

CSS rules are the styles that are applied on the HTML elements, such as font, images, and tables of a Web page. In other words, CSS is a combination of CSS rules that determines how a browser will display a Web page. A CSS rule consists of two parts, selector and declaration. The selector part describes the formatted element, such as headings, paragraphs, and id name; whereas, the code specified between the curly braces ({}) is the declaration part.

The following is an example of a CSS rule:
h1 {background-color: #00ff00}

In this preceding example, h1 is the selector part, and the {background-color: #00ff00} is the declaration part. Each declaration part is further divided into two parts, property and value. In the preceding example, background-color is a property and #00ff00 is its value.

As already learned, a CSS file is a combination of CSS rules that can be placed either in an external style sheet or in the head of an HTML document. If the CSS file is specified as an external file, the included CSS rules can be applied to all the HTML documents that are linked to the style sheet. Therefore, any changes made in the CSS file are automatically updated in all the linked HTML documents.

CSS rules can be placed in the following locations:
External CSS: Specifies that all CSS rules are collectively stored in the separate, external CSS files with the .css extension.
Internal CSS: Specifies that CSS rules are stored in a style tag in the head portion of the associated HTML document.
Inline style: Specifies the CSS code that resides within specific instances of tags throughout an HTML document.

Cascading Styles

In Dreamweaver, one of the most powerful aspects of CSS is the manner in which you can use it to make global style changes across an entire website. The styles of a Web page, as displayed on a Web browser, are mainly controlled by three different sources: the style sheet created by the author of the page, the user's customized style selection, and the default style of the Web browser. The final appearance of the Web page depends on the combination of these three sources. Some Web browsers have their own default style sheets that control the display of Web pages. You can customize the setting of such Web browsers and adjust the display of a Web page.

Inheritance is another important feature of CSS. Most of the element properties on a Web page are inherited. For example, paragraph tags inherit the properties of body tags, and bulleted list tags inherit the properties of the paragraph tag.

Let us look at an example of a CSS rule:
```
body{
    font-family:Arial, Helvetica, sans-serif; font-style:italic;
}
```

The preceding CSS rule defines font style as Arial, Helvetica, sans-serif, and italic. The paragraph tag also appears in Arial, Helvetica, sans-serif, and italic because the paragraph tag appears under the body tag. If you want to be more specific with the paragraph tag, use the following rule:

```
body{
    font-family:Arial, Helvetica, sans-serif; font-style:italic;
}
P{
    font-family:Georgia, "Times New Roman", serif; font-style:oblique;
    font-size:9px;
}
```

In the preceding CSS rule, all the text under the body tag, except the paragraph text, appears in Arial, Helvetica, sans-serif, and italic. The paragraph text appears in Georgia, "Times New Roman", Times, serif, and oblique, and 9px. Technically, the paragraph text first inherits the properties that are set for the body text, but then ignores them because it has properties of its own. Now we will discuss about shorthand CSS properties.

Shorthand CSS Properties
Dreamweaver provides the CSS specification to create styles by using an abbreviated syntax, known as shorthand CSS. You can define the values of various properties, such as text, images, and tables of a Web page by using a single declaration in shorthand CSS property. Consider the following CSS code:

```
body{
    font-family:Arial, Helvetica, sans-serif;
    font-style:italic;
    font-variant :normal;
    font-size:9px;
    line-height:auto;
    font-weight:100;
    font-stretch:normal;
    font-size-adjust:inherit;
}
```

In the preceding CSS code, you can see that the values of the font appear with the font properties. The same code can be written in the shorthand CSS property as follows:

```
body{ font: Arial, Helvetica, sans-serif italic 9px auto 100 inherit }
```

In the preceding code, you can see that the values of the font are declared in the declaration part without defining the font properties. When you use the shorthand CSS property, the omitted values are automatically assigned their default values. Therefore, the preceding shorthand CSS property omits the font-variant, font-stretch, and font-size-adjust tags.

Working with the CSS STYLES Panel

The CSS STYLES panel displays all the CSS rules and properties that can be used in a Web page. You can use the CSS STYLES panel to modify the CSS properties of a single Web page or all the Web pages. In this section of the lesson, you will explore: CSS STYLES panel modes, CSS STYLES panel buttons, and CSS STYLES preferences.

Describing the CSS STYLES Panel Modes

The CSS STYLES panel contains two modes, All and Current. You can switch between these two modes, depending on the requirement. Using the CSS STYLES panel, you can modify CSS properties, such as style or ID. By default, the CSS STYLES panel appears at the right side of Dreamweaver workspace, as shown in picture 4.3.

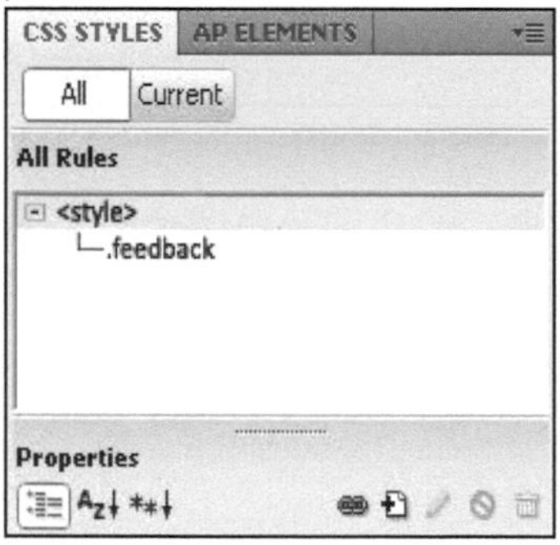

Picture 4.3 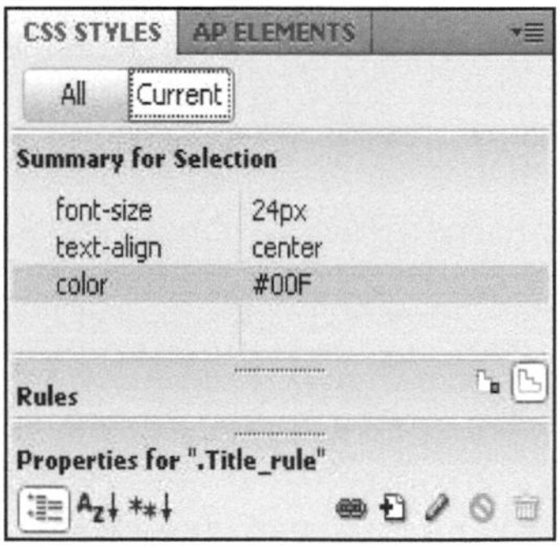   Picture 4.4

As you can see in picture 4.3, the All mode is divided into two panes:
All Rules: Displays every embedded and external style rule associated with the current Web page.
Properties: Allows you to edit CSS properties for any selected rule in the All Rules pane. Any changes you make in the Properties pane are immediately applied to the current Web page.

The Current mode (shown in picture 4.4) displays three panes:
Summary for Selection: Displays the CSS properties for the current selection in the document.
Rules: Displays the location of the selected properties.
Properties: Allows you to edit CSS properties for the rule defining the selection.

Describing the CSS STYLES Panel Buttons

As showing in picture 4.3, the CSS STYLES panel contains the following seven types of buttons at the bottom pane:

Show Category View: Displays the properties in a grouped manner. The groups are Font, Background, Block, Border, Box, List, Positioning, Extensions, Tables, Content, and Quotes. Each group contains a list that you can expand or collapse by clicking the Plus (+) button next to the group name.
Show List View: Displays all the properties in an alphabetical order.
Show only Set Properties: Displays only those properties that have been set in the selected CSS rule.
Attach Style Sheet: Displays the Attach External Style Sheet dialog box from where you can browse a style sheet to link to or to import it in your document.
New CSS Rule: Displays the New CSS Rule dialog box, where you can create a new CSS rule, such as HTML tag and CSS selector.
Edit Style: Displays a dialog box to edit the styles in the current Web page or in an external style sheet.
Delete CSS Rule: Deletes the selected CSS rule or property from the CSS STYLES panel.

Setting CSS Style Preferences

CSS style preferences control how Dreamweaver writes code to define CSS STYLES. These can be written In a shorthand as well as longhand form. Setting CSS style preferences help you to write the code in the shorthand form. Let's perform the following steps to set the preferences for CSS STYLES:

1. **Open** a Web page that contains CSS rules or an external CSS file. In this case, you can open the **feedback.html** Web page.

2. Choose **Edit> Preferences** from the Dreamweaver Menu bar. It opens the Preferences dialog box on your screen.

3. Select the **CSS Styles** option under the Category section. The options for the CSS Styles category appear under the CSS Styles section.
The Preferences dialog box for the CSS Styles section displays the following three groups:
When creating CSS rules: Controls the shorthand rules at the time of creating CSS rules. *transition*
When editing CSS rules: Controls the shorthand rules in the existing style sheet. *Acc to setting /open CSS*
When Double-clicking in CSS panel: Selects a tool for editing CSS rules. *Edit using CSS dialog*

4. You can select the check boxes and radio buttons beside the desired options to apply the required setting. For now, **select** the Font check box.

5. **Click** the OK button to save the settings. The CSS Styles now enables the shorthand form for the Font option. After setting the Preferences dialog box, let's learn how to create a new CSS rule.

Lesson 12
Introducing Cascading Style Sheets
You can create a new CSS rule for your Web page to format HTML tags or a range of text indentified by a class attributes. When you create a new CSS rule, the new CSS Rule definition dialog box appears. The CSS Rule definition dialog box contains different categories of options, which you can use to define a CSS

rule. Some commonly used categories of the CSS Rule definition dialog box are Type (for specifying fonts), Background (for specifying the background color of the Web page), and Border (for specifying outlines in the Web page). So in this lesson, you will learn to describe the categories in the CSS Rule definition dialog box, edit a CSS rule, add a property to CSS rule, and move a CSS rule.

To work with a CSS rule, you need to create a CSS rule first. Let us perform the following steps to create a new CSS rule:

1. **Open** the Web page **feedback.html** to create a new CSS rule. Then choose **Format> CSS Styles> New** from the Menu bar to open the New CSS Rule dialog box.

2. Enter the name: **Font_rule** under Selector Name for the option Choose or enter a name for your selector. Click the **OK** button after that.

It opens the **CSS Rule definition for .Font_rule** dialog box, as shown in picture 4.5. In this dialog box, you can define the properties for CSS rules, such as text font, background image and color, spacing and layout properties, and the appearance of list elements.

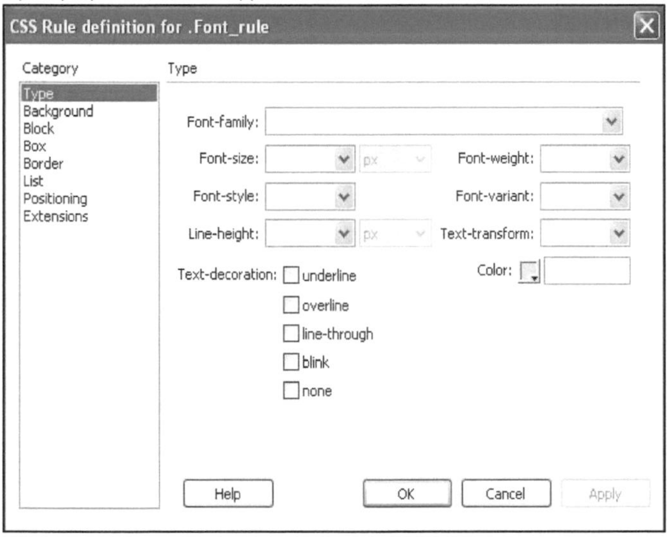

Picture 4.5

3. In Type section, select **"Times New Roman", Times, serif** for the Font-family option. For Font-size, select **16**. Select **orange** color from the Color option, and click the **OK** button at the bottom. The dialog box gets closed and the rule with the name, Font_rule is created.

4. **Select** the desired text in the feedback.html Web page to apply the CSS rule. After selecting the text, choose **Format> CSS Styles> Fontrule** to apply the CSS style. The rule named, **Font_rule** is applied to the selected text.

5. You can repeat the step 4 for applying the Font_rule to other HTML elements according to your requirement. Then select File> Save to save the changes made to the feedback.html Web page. After that, select File> Preview in Browser> IExplore to preview the Web page in Internet Explorer.

Describing the Categories in the CSS Rule Definition Dialog Box

The CSS Rule definition dialog box provides access to all of the formatting options available with regard to the text and graphics of your Web page. The different categories available in the CSS Rules definition dialog box are as follows: Type, Background, Block, Box, Border, List, Positioning, and Extensions. Now let us explore these categories.

The Type Category

The Type category in the CSS Rule definition dialog box defines basic font and type settings for a CSS style. The options available in the Type category are as follows:

Font-family: Sets the font family for a CSS rule.
Font-size: Defines the size of the text. Use the dropdown arrow to select from a list of options that include pixels, picas, and percentages.
Font-weight: Controls the appearance of the text by using the specific or relative boldness option.
Font-style: Selects the font style. It specifies Normal, Italic, and Oblique as the font style. The default setting is Normal.
Font-variant: Selects a variation of the font, such as normal or small caps.
Line-height: Specifies the height of a line on which the text is placed.
Text-transform: Capitalizes the first letter of each word in the selection or sets the text to all uppercase or lowercase.
Text-decoration: Allows you to decorate the text with various effects, such as underline, overline, or line-through to the text. By default setting for regular text is None and Underline for links.
Color: Selects the color of the text.

The Background Category

The Background category in the CSS Rule definition dialog box defines how the background of a Web page is displayed. The options in the Background category are as follows:

Background-color: Specifies the background color of an element, such as table. You can click the color palette and select predefined colors or create custom colors to use as the background color.
Background-image: Selects a background image as a part of the style definition. You can click the Browse button to select the image.
Background-repeat: Determines whether or not the background image is repeated and how it is repeated. The Background-repeat options are as follows:
- **no-repeat:** Displays the background image once, without repeating it horizontally or vertically behind the element.
- **repeat:** Repeats the background image vertically and horizontally behind an element.
- **repeat-x:** Repeats the background image horizontally, but not vertically, behind the element.
- **repeat-y:** Repeats the background image vertically instead of horizontally, behind the element.

Background-attachment: Determines the behavior of the background when the Web page is scrolled and offers following two settings:
- **fixed:** Fixes the background to one place in the viewing area and does not scroll out of sight even when the Web page is scrolled.
- **scroll:** Scrolls the background along with the Web page. This option is the default behavior for background.

Background-position (X): Aligns the image left, center, or right.
Background-position (Y): Aligns the image top, center, or bottom.

The Block Category

The Block category in the CSS Rule definition dialog box defines the spacing and alignment settings for tags and attributes. The following options are available in the Block category:

Word-spacing: Specifies the amount of white-space inserted between words in points, millimeters, centimeters, picas, inches, pixels, em, ex, and percentage.

Note: 1em is a unit of measurement that is equal to the current size of a font. 2em means 2 times the size of the current font. For example, if an element is displayed with a font size of 12 points, then 2em is 24 points. On the other hand, 1 ex is the x-height or a font. The x-height is usually about half the font size. For example, if an element is displayed with a font size of 14 points, then 1 ex is 7 points.

Letter-spacing: Specifies the amount of white-space inserted between letters in points, millimeters, centimeters, picas, inches, pixels, em, and ex.
Vertical-align: Specifies the alignment of inline elements, such as text and images, in relation to the elements that surround them. Note that you may have to preview a Web page in a browser to see these effects. The options to do so are, baseline, sub, super, top, text-top, middle, bottom, and text-bottom.
Text-align: Sets the alignment of text to left, right, center, or justify.
Text-indent: Allows you to set the indent space for the first line of the text.
White-space: Determines how the white-space inside a block element is displayed. The options in the White-space dropdown list include:
- **Normal:** Removes any extra white-space.
- **Pre (for preformatted):** Leaves the white-spaces unchanged.
- **Nowrap:** Wraps text only when the code contains the line break (br) tag.

Display: Shows how to render an element in the browser. You can hide an element by selecting the none option.

The Box Category

The Box category in the CSS Rule definition dialog box defines the settings for tags and attributes that control the placement and appearance of elements on a Web page. The following options are available in the Box category:

Width: Specifies the width to use in style for images, <div> tags, or any other elements with specific dimensions. You can use pixels, points, inches, centimeters, millimeters, picas, em, ex, or percentages as units of measurements.

Height: Specifies the height to use in style for images, <div> tags, or any other elements that have their dimensions specified. You can use pixels, points, inches, centimeters, millimeters, picas, em, ex, or percentages as units of measurements.

Float: Specifies the alignment of a boxed element to the left or right so that other elements, such as text, wraps around it.

Clear: Prevents floating content from overlapping an area to the left or right, or both sies.

Padding: Sets the amount for the space (measured in pixels, centimeters, inches, points, etc.) around an element to its edge.

Margin: Sets the amount of space between the edge of an element and the other elements on a Web page. You can set the margins separately for the top, right, bottom, and left. Padding is measured in pixels, points, inches, centimeters, millimeters, picas, ems, exs, and percentage.

The Border Category

The Border category in the CSS Rule definition dialog box defines the settings, such as style, width, and color, for the borders around the elements on a Web page. The following options are available in the Border category:

Style: Sets the style appearance of the border.

Same for all: Sets the same border style properties to the Top, Right, Bottom, and Left of the element to which it is applied.

Width: Sets the thickness of an element's border.

Color: Sets the color of the border.

The List Category

The List category in the CSS Rule definition dialog box defines the settings, such as bullet size and type, for list tags. The following options are available in the List category:

List-style-type: Specifies bullet styles, such as disc, circle, square, decimal, lower-roman, upper-roman, upper-alpha, lower-alpha, or none.

List-style-image: Specifies a custom image for bullets. If you want to use a custom bullet, you can use the Browser button to locate an image and use it as a bullet.

List-style-Position: Specifies whether an item list or text wraps to the left margin.

The Positioning Category

The Positioning category of the CSS Rule definition dialog box defines how the content related to the selected CSS style is positioned on a Web page. The following options are available in the Positioning category:

Position: Specifies the position of an element, such as <div> tag as absolute, relative, fixed, or static:

- **Absolute:** Uses the top and left coordinates to control the position of an element relative to the upper-left corner of the browser window or the upper-left corner of an element containing the element. For example, the positioning of an AP Div element contained within another AP Div element is based on the position of the first AP Div element.
- **Fixed:** Positions an element relative to the top-left corner of the browser. The content of an element in fixed positioning remains constant even if the user scrolls down or across the page.
- **Relative:** Uses a position relative to the point where you insert the element into the Web page or relative to its container.

- **Static:** Places the content at its location in the text flow. This is the default option for the elements when no position type is selected.

Visibility: Controls the initial display settings of the element. The various visibility options are as follows:

- **Inherit:** Forces the layer to inherit the visibility property of the layer's parent. If no parent exists, the layer is visible.
- **Visible:** Displays the layer's content, regardless of a parent's visibility value.
- **Hidden:** Hides the layer's contents, regardless of a person's visibility value.

Width: Specifies a width to use in the styles applied to images, AP Divs, or any other elements that have their dimensions specified. You can use pixels, points, inches, centimeters, millimeters, picas, ems, exs, or percentages as units of measurements.

Height: Specifies a height to use in the styles applied to images, AP Divs, or any other elements that have their dimensions specified.

Z-index: Determines the stacking order of content. Elements with a higher Z-index appear above the elements of a lower Z-index.

Overflow: Determines how the browser displays the content of an element if the element does not contain the entire content. The various overflow options, are as follows:

- **Visible:** Forces an element to increase in size to display all its contents. The element expands downward and to the right.
- **Hidden:** Cuts off the content of the element that does not fit. This option does not provide scroll bars.
- **Scroll:** Adds scroll bars to an element regardless of whether or not the content exceed the size of the element.
- **Auto:** Displays scroll bars only when an element's contents exceed its boundaries. (This feature does not currently appear in the Dreamweaver workspace).

Placement: Defines the size and location of an element within its containing element. For example, you can set the right edge of the element to line up with the right edge of the element that contains it. You can use pixels points, inches, centimeters, millimeters, picas, ems, exs, or percentages.

- **Clip:** Sets the visible portion of the element through the top, right, bottom, and left attributes.

The Extensions Category

The Extensions category in the CSS Rule definition dialog box defines how content related to the selected CSS style is positioned on a Web page. The following options are available in the Extensions category:

Page break: Inserts a point in a Web page for a page break. This option allows you to control the way a document is printed.

Cursor: Defines the type of cursor that appears when you move the cursor over an element.

Filter: Enables you to apply special effects, such as drop shadows and motion blurs, to the elements. These effects are visible only in Internet Explorer.

Editing a CSS Rule

In Dreamweaver, you can easily edit CSS rules from an internal or external CSS file. When you edit a CSS file that controls the text in your Web page, you instantly reformat all the text controlled by the CSS file. In addition, if you edit an external style sheet, it affects all the documents linked the external style sheet. Perform the following simple steps to edit a CSS rule in the CSS STYLES panel:

1. **Open** a Web page (feedback.html), which consists of the CSS rule that you created in the previous section of this lesson. Here you will edit the same CSS rule of this page.

2. Click the **Current** button which is in the <u>Panel Group</u> under <u>CSS STYLES</u> tab (already shown in picture 1.7). After you click, it displays the options present in the Current mode.

3. Double-click the **font** property in Current mode. It opens the **CSS Rule definition for .Font_rule** dialog box.

4. Select the required property to edit. For now, you can select to edit the **Font-family** by changing the family of the font to **Comic Sans MS, cursive**.

5. Click the **OK** button to apply the changes. You will see that the new family of font **Comic Sans MS, cursive,** is applied to the text in the Web page. Then, select File> Save to save the changes.

Adding a Property to CSS Rule

Dreamweaver allows you to add new properties to a CSS rule in the CSS STYLES panel. You can do this by performing the following steps:

1. **Drag** the CSS STYLES panel to <u>increase</u> its size by dragging the double-point arrow at the top right corner. It is shown in picture 4.6 with the red arrow.

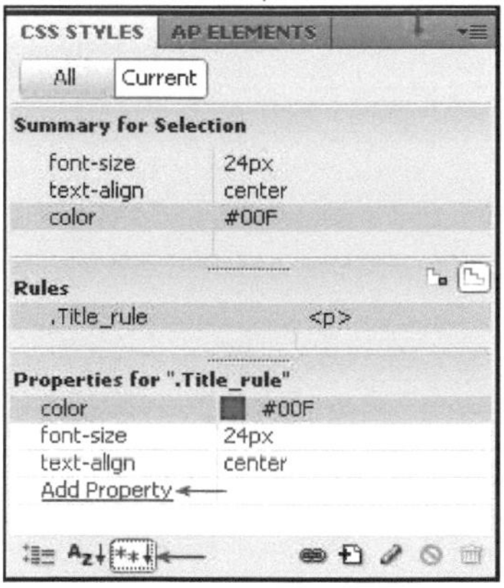

Picture 4.6 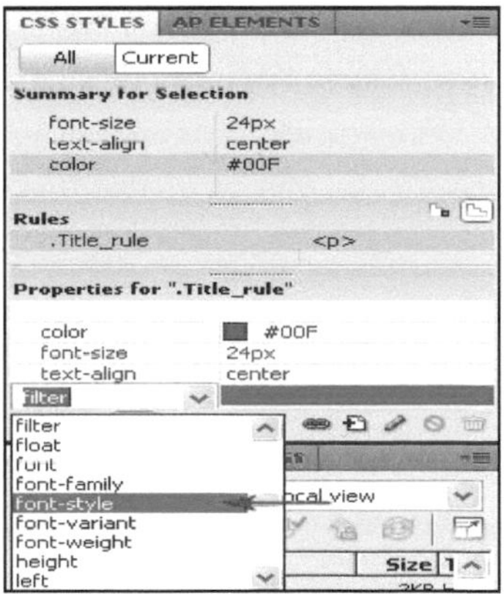   Picture 4.7

2. **Click** the button that says **Show only set properties** at the bottom. This is the third button at the bottom (shown in picture 4.6 with a red arrow).

3. Click the **Add Property** link which is visible now. It is also shown in the picture 4.6 with a red arrow. When you click it, a list box appears, as shown in picture 4.7.

4. **Click** the down arrow in the list box. Then you need to select the **font-style** property in the list, as shown in picture 4.7). The selected property appears in the Add Property column.

5. **Select** the value of the property from the list box beside the new property. For now, you can select the **Italic** property. It makes the font-style italic in the Web page.

Moving a CSS Rule

You can easily move the CSS rules to different locations in Dreamweaver, for example, from one Web page to another Web page or from one Web page to an external style sheet. Here are the steps to perform:

1. Click the **All** button under CSS STYLES in Panel Group. Then you need to right-click the **Font_rule** that you will move. It opens a context menu on the screen.

2. Select the **Move CSS Rules** option from the context menu. It opens the Move to External Style Sheet dialog box. This dialog box allows you to move the desired CSS rule either to a new external style sheet or to an existing external style sheet.

3. **Select** the radio button that says **A new style sheet**. Then click the **OK** button, which opens the **Save Style Sheet File As** dialog box.

4. **Type** the name of the new CSS file in the File name text box. For now, you can type the name as **Reference_styleSheet**.

5. Click the **Save** button to save the new style sheet. You will see that the selected CSS rule moves to the specified new style sheet, and the new CSS file opens in the Dreamweaver workspace. Choose **File> Close** to close the feedback.html Web page.

Lesson 13
Working with External CSS Style Sheets

In Dreamweaver, an external style sheet enables you to create styles that you can apply to all the Web pages throughout a website. To apply an external style sheet, you store the style sheet information in a separate CSS file, which can be linked to any Web page. You can define styles for common formatting options used in the entire site, such as headings, captions, and even images, which makes applying multiple formatting options to elements fast and easy. In this lesson, you will learn to create an external style sheet, link an external style sheet to a Web page, edit a CSS style sheet, use the Design-Time style sheet, use sample Dreamweaver style sheets, and format the CSS code.

Creating an External Style Sheet

You can create external style sheets just as you create internal style sheets in the HTML documents, except that external style sheets need to be saved as a separate .css file. When you use Dreamweaver to create an external style sheet, Dreamweaver automatically links the style sheet to the Web page you are working on. You can then link it to any other Web page in which you want to apply the style definitions. Perform the following steps to create an external style sheet:

1. **Open** the Web page where you want to link a new external style sheet. In our case, we open the already created **Tips.html** Web page.

2. Choose **Format> CSS Styles> New** to open the New CSS Rule dialog box. Then in this dialog box, **select** the option: **Tag (redefines an HTML element)** from the list box under the Selector Type category.

3. Under Selector Name category, select: **body** option from the list box. Then under Rule Definition category, select: **(New Style Sheet File)** option to define the placement of the rule.

4. Click the **OK** button which will open the Save Style Sheet File As dialog box. In this dialog box, **type** the name of the style sheet as: **body_rule** in the File name text box.

5. Set the **Style Sheet Files (*.css)** option in the Save as type list box. Then click the **Save** button at the bottom. It opens the CSS Rule Definition for body in body rule.css dialog box. Using this dialog box, you can define the new style rule specifying all the formatting options that you want to apply with the new style rule.

6. **Select** the font family: **"Comic Sans MS", cursive** option from the Font-family. Then select the Font-size: **12**, Font-weight: **normal**, Font-style: **normal**, and Font-variant: **small-caps**.

7. Click the **OK** button to apply the specified formatting settings. The CSS Rule Definition dialog box closes. The new style is saved to your external style sheet and the new external style sheet appears in the Dreamweaver workspace.

8. Select **File> Save** to save the changes. Now that you know how to create an external style sheet, you need to learn how to link an external style sheet to a Web page.

Linking to an External Style Sheet
Dreamweaver automatically makes any new external style sheet available to a new Web page by attaching the style sheet. You can attach any external style sheet to the Web page with the Attach Style Sheet command in the CSS STYLES panel. Do these steps to link an external style sheet to a Web page:

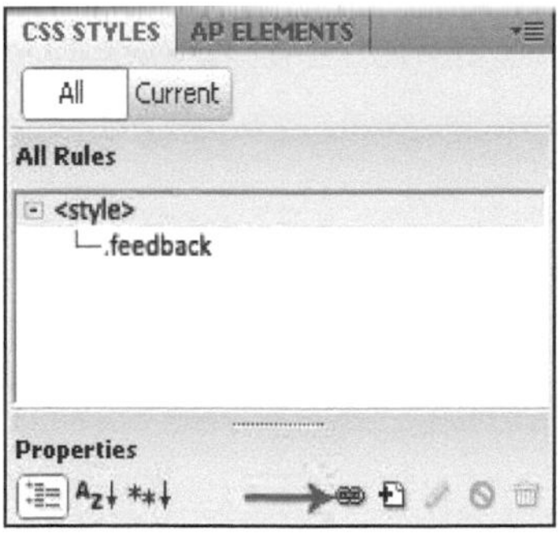

1. **Open** the Web page **Articles.html** to link an external style sheet.

2. Click the **Attach Style Sheet** button at the lower-right part of the CSS STYLES panel, as shown in picture 4.8 with a red arrow. It opens the Attach External Style Sheet dialog box.

3. Click the **Browse** button beside the **File/URL** combo box to locate the CSS file. It opens the Select Style Sheet File dialog box.

4. Select the style sheet **body_rule** and click the **OK** button at the bottom.

Picture 4.8

The **Select Style Sheet File** dialog box closes and the **Attach External Style Sheet** dialog box appears on your screen. You can select the **Link** radio button to attach the style sheet to an HTML document by linking it, or select the **Import** radio button to add a reference of one style sheet to another. In addition, you can select an option from the Media dropdown list to specify the use for the style sheet. You can leave this option blank if you are attaching a style sheet to control the way a Web page will appear in the Web browser or if you have created the style sheet that formats your Web page for printing.

5. **Click** the OK button to close the Attach External Style Sheet dialog box. You will see on your screen that the external CSS file is automatically linked to the Web page.

Editing a CSS Style Sheet

You can edit CSS rules in CSS by either using the CSS STYLES panel or directly editing the rules in the CSS file. Perform the following steps to edit the rules in a CSS file by using the CSS STYLES panel:

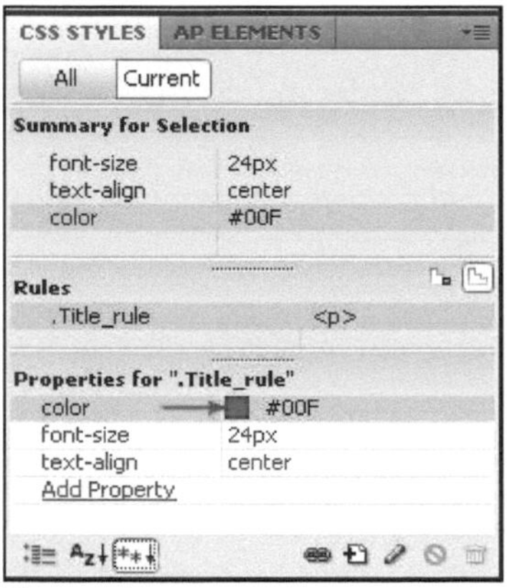

1. **Open** the external CSS file **body_rule.css** in which you want to make changes. Then click the **color** property, as shown in picture 4.9 with the red arrow. It opens the color palette.

2. Select the **red** color. You will see on your screen that the green color of the font is changed to red.

3. Click the desired file tab to open the file that consists of the rule that we have edited in the preceding steps. In our case, we **click** the **Articles.html** file tab at the top left hand corner below Menu bar. You will see that the font color is changed to red.

4. Choose **File**> **Save All** to save the changes made to all the Web pages.

Picture 4.9

Using Design-Time Style Sheets

The Design-Time style sheets feature of Dreamweaver allows you to view how different external style sheets will affect a Web page, without actually linking them. These style sheets affect only the appearance of styles in Dreamweaver. The styles that are actually attached to or embedded in the Web page appear in a browser. As Design-Time style sheets are not linked, they are displayed only at runtime when the Web page opens in Dreamweaver. Perform the following steps to use a Design-Time style sheet:

1. **Open** the Articles.html Web page in which you want to use a Design-Time style sheet. Then select **Format**> **CSS Styles**> **Design-time**. It opens the Design-Time Style Sheets dialog box.

2. In the Design-Time Style Sheets dialog box, click the **+ button** which is just above the Show only at design time option. This option will add the required style sheet. It opens the Select File dialog box.

3. **Select** the style sheet that you want to show at design time. In our case, we select the style sheet, **Reference_styleSheet**, and click the **OK** button. The Select File dialog box is closed and the selected style sheet appears in the Show only at design time text box.

*Similarly, you ca select the CSS file that you want to hide by suing the **Hide a design time** option. To remove a style sheet in the Show only at design time and Hide at design time options, select the style sheet and click the Minus (-) button of the respective option in the Design-Time Style Sheets dialog box.*

4. Click the **OK** button to set the style sheet and close the dialog box. The required style sheet appears in the CSS STYLES panel.

Using Sample Dreamweaver Style Sheets

Dreamweaver provides sample style sheets that you can apply to Web page or use them as the starting point to develop your own style sheets. Perform the following steps to use a sample Dreamweaver style sheet:

1. Click the **Attach Style Sheet** button in the lower-right corner of the CSS STYLES panel, as already shown in picture 4.8. It opens the Attach External Style Sheet dialog box.

2. At the bottom of the Attach External Style Sheet dialog box, click the **sample style sheets** link. It opens the Sample Style Sheets dialog box.

3. **Select** the desired style sheet from the list box. The preview pane displays the text and color formatting of the selected style sheet. In our case, we select the **Full Design: Verdana, Yellow/Green** style sheet.

4. In the same dialog box, click the **Browse** button at the bottom to navigate the location where you want to save this style sheet. It opens the Choose Local Folder dialog box.

5. Select the folder **Dreamweaver CS6** to save the sample style sheet. Then click the **Select** button. The Choose Local Folder dialog box closes and the Sample Style Sheets dialog box appears again on the screen.

6. Click the **OK** button to use the selected sample style sheet. The selected sample style sheet is applied to the Web page.

Formatting the CSS Code

Dreamweaver allows you to set the preferences that control the format of your CSS code when you create or edit a CSS rule by using the Dreamweaver workspace. When you set the preference for the CSS code, the preferences you select are automatically applied to all the new CSS rules that you create. You can also manually apply the preferences to individual documents. Perform the following steps to set the preferences for the CSS code:

1. **Open** the CSS file, whose code you want to format, in Dreamweaver. In our case, we open the **Reference_styleSheet.css** file.

2. Choose **Edit> Preferences** to open the <u>Preferences</u> dialog box. In this dialog box, select the **Code Format** option from the <u>Category</u> section. It opens the Code Format preference options in the right pane.

3. In the same Preferences dialog box, click the **CSS** button (which is beside Advanced Formatting option). It opens the <u>CSS Source Format Options</u> dialog box.

4. **Select** the **Opening brace on separate line** check box to place the opening braces for a CSS rule on separate lines. Then click the **OK** button after setting the options. The CSS Source Format Option dialog box gets closed.

5. Click the **OK** button of the <u>Preferences</u> dialog box. The CSS page appears in the Dreamweaver workspace as per the setting.

Lesson 14
Working with CSS Layouts
Although you can use any HTML element for the layout of a Web page, the <div> tag is used most often to create page layouts with CSS. The <div> tag is a container used to hold content or divide a Web page, separating one section of the page content from the other. Unlike other HTML tags, the <div> tag has no inherent formatting features. If CSS is applied to a <div> tag that is empty, the <div> tag will not appear on a Web page. When you create a style that corresponds to a <div> tag, you can specify properties, such as alignment, border, margin, height, and width to control how the <div> tag is displayed on the Web page. In this lesson, you will learn about the CSS layout, and how to create a Web page by using a CSS layout.

Defining a CSS Layout
A CSS layout uses the CSS format rather than traditional HTML tables and frames, to organize the content of a Web page. The <div> tags are the basic building blocks of the CSS layout. While creating CSS layouts, you place the <div> tags on the page, add content to the <div> tags, and position them in appropriate places. You can position the <div> tags absolutely by defining the x and y coordinates or relatively by defining their distance from the other elements in the Web page.

Creating a Web Page using a CSS Layout
In Dreamweaver, using the predesigned CSS layouts is the easiest way to create a Web page with the CSS layout. You can also create a CSS layout by using Dreamweaver's absolutely-positioned elements, which are also known as AP elements. These are simply <div> tags with absolute positions assigned to them.

While creating a new page in Dreamweaver, you can use a sample CSS layout provided by Dreamweaver. You can also create your own CSS layout as per your requirement. Perform the following steps to create a Web page with a CSS layout:

1. Choose **File> New** to create a new document. The <u>New Document</u> dialog box appears on the Dreamweaver screen.

2. **Select** the required layout from the Layout list box. In our case, we select the **2 column liquid, left sidebar, header and footer** layout. The predesigned CSS layout contains the following types of columns:

Fixed: Specifies the column width in pixels. The column does not resize based on the browser.
Liquid: Specifies the column width as a percentage of width of the Web browser used by a site visitor.

3. Click the **Attach Style Sheet** button which is at the right side in lower-middle beside the Attach CSS file option to attach a CSS file to your new page. It opens the Attach External Style Sheet dialog box.

4. Click the **browse** button to select the style sheet that you want to attach. In our case, we select the **Level3_3.css** style sheet. Then click the **OK** button.

5. Click the **Create** button to create the new Web page. The new Web page appears on the screen. Then select **File> Save** to save the Web page. It opens the Save As dialog box.

6. **Browse** to the location **Dreamweaver CS6** folder. Then you need to type the name of the Web page as: **CSS layout**, and click the **Save** button. The Web page is saved with CSS layout name.

Working with AP Div Element

The AP element is an HTML page element. Specifically, it is a <div> tag that has an absolute position assigned to it. AP element also contains text, images, and other content that you insert in the body of the HTML document. These elements are used for laying out Web pages. In Dreamweaver, you can place AP elements one on the other to hide some AP elements while performing various functions, such as showing other AP elements, moving an AP element across the browser, and adding a background image in an AP element.

Dreamweaver creates AP elements using the <div> tag. When you draw an AP element using the Draw AP Div tool, Dreamweaver inserts a <div> tag in the HTML code of the Web page, and assigns the tag an id value. For example, id value apDiv1 for the first AP Div, id value apDiv2 for the second AP Div, and so on. You can rename the AP Div as per the requirement by using the AP ELEMENTS panel or the PROPERTIES inspector. In this section of the lesson, you learn how to insert an AP Div element, draw multiple AP Div elements, set preferences for an AP Div element, and set the properties for an AP Div element. You also get an overview of the AP ELEMENTS panel, and learn to edit AP Div elements. Let's start with inserting an AP Div element in a Dreamweaver document.

Inserting an AP Div Element

In Dreamweaver, you can create an AP element by using <div> tags. When you draw an AP element by using the Draw AP Div tool, Dreamweaver automatically inserts a <div> tag in the document and assigns the default div name and id value to it. Dreamweaver also uses embedded CSS in the head of the document to position and assign the AP Div element using appropriate dimensions. Perform the following steps to draw an AP Div element:

1. **Create** a new blank HTML document in Dreamweaver workspace. Then select **Insert> Layout Objects> AP Div** from the Menu bar. A box representing an AP Div appears at the top of the page outlined in blue, as shown in picture 5.0.

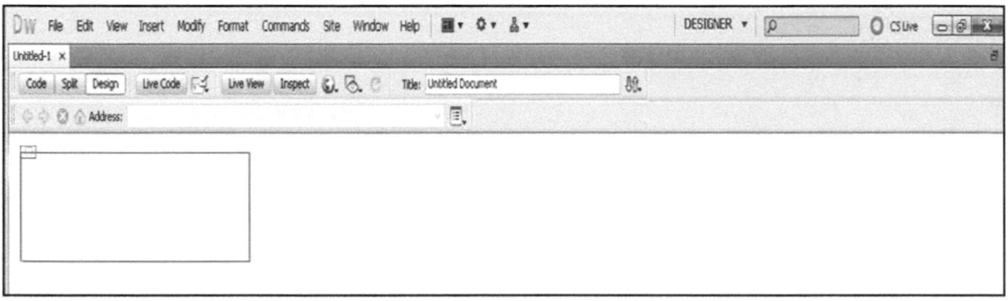

Picture 5.0

2. **Hold** the mouse-pointer over the outline of the AP Div element. The cursor turns into a four-pointed arrow. Then **drag** any of the handles to resize the AP Div element. When resized, the AP Div element looks as shown in picture 5.1.

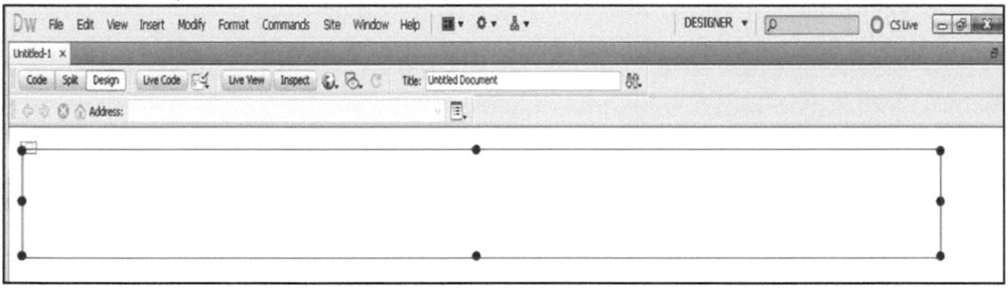

Picture 5.1

Drawing Multiple AP Div Elements Consecutively
In Dreamweaver, you can draw more than one AP Div elements consecutively. You can also draw nested AP Div elements by dragging the mouse-pointer inside the parent AP Div elements, in the same manner. In case, if the INSERT panel is not visible in the Dreamweaver workspace, you can make the panel visible by clicking Window> Insert from the Menu bar. Now perform the following steps to draw multiple AP Div elements consecutively:

1. **Click** the down arrow button in the Common dropdown list and select the **Layout** option from the dropdown, as shown in picture 5.2. It opens a list of layout options in the INSERT panel.

2. Select the **Draw AP** Div option from the list. Then press the **Ctrl** key on the keyboard, and **drag** the mouse-pointer to draw multiple AP Div elements consecutively.

You may continue to draw new AP Div elements as long as you do not release the Ctrl key. In our case, we have drawn 4 AP Div elements, as shown in picture 5.3 below.

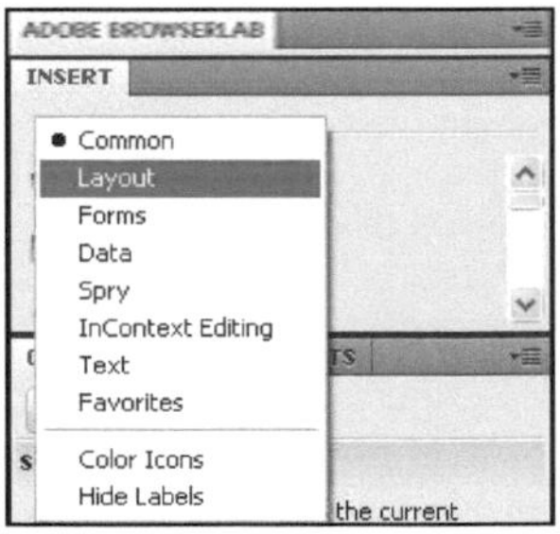

Picture 5.2

Teach Yourself Adobe Dreamweaver CS6 – By Niranjan Jha – Published by Cromosys

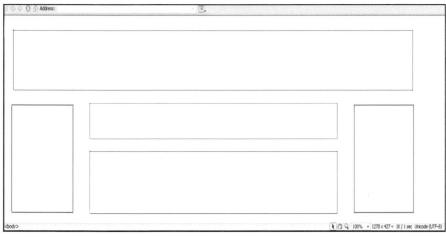

Picture 5.3

3. **Release** the mouse-pointer at the end. You will see that multiple AP Div elements are drawn in the Dreamweaver workspace.

Setting Preferences of AP Div Element

You can use the AP Div elements category in the Preference dialog box to define the default settings for the new AP Div elements that you create. Do these steps to set the preferences for an AP Div element:

1. Select **Edit> Preferences** from the Menu bar to open the Preferences dialog box. Using this dialog box, you can set the desired setting for the AP Div elements that you create.

2. Click the **AP Elements** option from the Category section. The following options appear in the Preferences dialog box:

Visibility: Determines whether the AP Div elements are visible or not. After clicking the down arrow button, the options that appear are default, inherit, visible, and hidden.
Width: Specifies the width of the AP Div elements.
Height: Specifies the height of the AP Div elements.
Background color: Specifies the background color of the AP Div element. You can select a color from the color palette for your AP Div element.
Background image: Specifies the background image for the AP Div element. You can click the Browse button to select the image file for the background image.
Nesting: Determines whether an AP Div that you draw inside an existing AP Div should be a nested AP Div or not. The **Nest when created within an AP div** check box specifies whether or not an AP Div that you draw starting from a point within the boundaries of an existing AP Div should be a nested AP Div. Hold down the Alt key on the keyboard to temporarily change the settings while drawing an AP Div.

3. **Click** the down arrow of <u>Background</u> color to open the color palette. Then **select** the desired (blue) color to fill as the background color for the AP Div elements.

4. Click the **OK** button to save the settings. The settings of the AP Elements category in the Preferences dialog box for the AP Div elements are automatically applied to the new AP Div elements you create.

5. **Draw** an AP Div element on the Dreamweaver workspace. You will see on your screen that the specified setting is applied.

Setting Properties of AP Div Element

Similar to other HTML elements, AP Div elements have various attributes in the PROPERTIES inspector. When you select an AP Div element, its attributes appear in the PROPERTIES inspector. The following is a brief description of the properties that you can set from the PROPERTIES inspector:

CSS-P element: Defines the ID name for the selected AP Div element. This ID name identifies the AP Div elements. You can only use the alphanumeric characters rather than the spaces, hyphens, slashes, or periods. Every AP Div element must have a unique ID.

L and T: Specifies the position of the AP Div element by taking the upper-left corner of the AP Div element, relative to the upper-left corner of the Web page.

W and H: Specifies the width and height, respectively, of the AP Div element.

Z-index: Specifies the Z-index or stacking order of the AP Div elements. In the browser, the AP Div element with a higher Z-index appears over the AP Div element with a lower Z-index. Therefore, the Z-index provides an easy way to change the stacking order of AP Div elements.

Vis: Specifies whether the AP Div elements are initially visible. You can click the down arrow button and select the desired option from the Vis dropdown list.

Bg image: Specifies the background image for the AP Div element. You can click the Browser button to select the background image.

Bg color: Specifies the background color for the AP Div element. You can click the color palette and set the desired color.

Class: Applies a custom CSS style to the AP element from an internally or externally linked CSS.

Overflow: Determines how the AP Div elements appear in the browser when the content exceeds the AP Div element's specified size. You can click the down arrow button and select the following desired option.

Visible: Specifies that if extra content appear in the AP Div element, the AP Div element stretches to accommodate it.

Hidden: Hides the extra content in the browser.

Scroll: Allows the browser to add the scroll bar to the AP Div element.

Auto: Allows the browser to display the scroll bar only when the AP Div element is needed.

Clip: Specifies the left, right, top, and bottom coordinates to define a rectangle in the coordinate space of the AP Div element. After defining the coordinates, the AP Div element is clipped and only the specified region is visible.

Perform the following steps to set the properties of an AP Div element by using the PROPERTIES inspector:

1. **Select** the AP Div element on the Web page whose properties you want to change. For now you can select the first AP Div element drawn on the Web page.

2. In the PROPERTIES inspector, click the **Browse for File** button to browse for the image. This option is at the right side of Bg image option (and behind Class option). After clicked, it opens the Select Image Source dialog box.

3. **Browse** to the location where you have an image saved in your hard drive. Then **select** the image, and click the **OK** button.

If the image selected by you is not saved at the root folder (Dreamweaver CS6 folder), then a message box appears asking you to copy the image in the root folder.

4. Click the **Yes** button on the message box. It opens the Copy File As dialog box. Then **type** the desired name (in the File name text box) of the image with which you want to save the image.

5. Click the **Save** button on the Copy File As dialog box. The desired image is inserted as a background in the selected AP Div element.

The PROPERTIES inspector for multiple AP Div elements has some extra properties options than those available in the PROPERTIES inspector for a single AP Div element. To select more than one AP Div element in the document, press the Shift key on the keyboard and select the AP Div elements. After selecting the AP Div elements, the properties for the AP Div elements appear in the PROPERTIES inspector. The only extra option is the Tag option, which shows the HTML tag used to define the AP elements. You can click the down arrow and select the desired option for the Tag from the list.

Exploring the AP Div Elements Panel Overview

The AP ELEMENTS panel appears in the CSS STYLES panel at the right side of the Dreamweaver workspace, which shows the order of AP Div elements. You can use the AP ELEMENTS panel to prevent overlaps, change the visibility, stack order, and position of nested AP Div elements, and select one or more AP Div elements. In the AP ELEMENTS panel, the names of the AP Div elements are displayed in a list according to the value of the Z-index. By default, the AP Div elements created first appear at the bottom of the list and the newly created AP Div elements appear at the top of the list. In this section, you learn to change the stacking order of AP Div elements, and change the visibility of AP Div element.

Changing the Stacking Order of AP Div Elements

In HTML code, the stacking order or Z-index of the AP Div elements determines the order in which they are created in a browser. The higher the Z-index of an AP Div element, the higher the AP Div element is in the stacking order. You can change the Z-index for each AP Div element by using the AP ELEMENTS panel or PROPERTIES inspector. For this, you need to type a number beside the Z-Index option in the PROPERTIES inspector. A high number moves the AP Div element up in the stacking order, while a low number moves the AP Div element down in the stacking order. You can also change the stack order of AP Div elements in the AP ELEMENTS panel by clicking the desired AP Div element and dragging the mouse-pointer up or down to change the stacking order. Now perform the following steps to change the stack order:

1. **Select** the required AP Div element. In our case, we select the **#apDiv4** element in the AP ELEMENTS panel.

2. **Drag** the selected AP Div element to the position where you want to place it. The selected AP Div element is moved to the Top position.

Changing the Visibility of AP Div Elements
While working with AP Div elements, you can select the AP Div elements you want to display or hide in the AP ELEMENTS panel. Perform the following steps to change the visibility of AP Div elements:

1. Click the **AP ELEMENTS** tab, which is beside the CSS STYLES tab in the Panel Group. You will see that the eye icon appears for every AP Div element. You can show or hide the AP Div element according to the requirement. An open eye means the AP Div element is visible, and a closed eye means the AP Div element is invisible.

2. **Click** the opened eye icon of the AP Div element that you want to hide. After clicked, the AP Div element is hidden.

Editing AP Div Elements
You can edit AP Div element in the document window of Dreamweaver. In other words, you can resize, move, and align the AP Div elements. You can resize the AP Div element by clicking the border of the AP Div element and placing the mouse pointer on any corner or region so that the mouse pointer turns into a two-arrow pointer. After this, drag the mouse pointer and set the size of the AP Div element. Alternatively, you can directly define the values in the PROPERTIES inspector for the width and height. You can also move the place of AP Div elements in the Design view of the document window in the same way you move objects in most basic graphics applications. If the Prevent check box is selected in the AP ELEMENTS panel, then you can move an AP Div element anywhere on the Document window. Alternatively, you can directly define the values in the PROPERTIES inspector for the width and height.

Lesson 15
Working with Dreamweaver Templates and Library Items
A template is a common structure that is used as a layout for the Web pages of a website. Usually, Web pages have a standard structure that consists of a header, a navigation bar, and a footer. This structure will be common for all the Web pages of the website. Now, let's suppose you have a website that consists of 25 Web pages and you want to add a new company logo on all the Web pages at the same location. To do that, you have to go to each Web page and add the logo manually. However, if you are using a template, all you need to do is add the logo on the template and the logo is added to all the Web pages automatically. In addition, templates enable you to control the sections on a Web page that can be edited as well as those that need to remain fixed across all the Web pages in a website.

You can also define elements of the Web pages that are used repetitively throughout your website in Dreamweaver. These elements are referred to as library items, such as slogans, copyright messages, or banners. After these elements are created, you can simply use them by just inserting from the ASSETS panel. Moreover, Dreamweaver enables the automatic update of all the instances of an element when the changes are made to it ASSETS panel. So in this lesson, you will have an overview of templates, including Editable Regions, Editable Optional Regions, and Repeating Regions. You will also learn to set tag attributes of a template, work with nested templates, and modify templates. In addition, you will learn to apply a template to an existing Web page, detach a template, export a template-based Web page, and work with library items. Let us begin with the overview of the templates available in Dreamweaver.

Exploring Dreamweaver Templates

Dreamweaver templates allow you to create and apply a consistent page design and layout across a website. Templates also help in maintaining a website, as changes to the elements of a Web page may be used to globally update the Web pages of the associated website. A template allows you to define the overall layout of the Web pages of a website, and typically contains elements that consistently appear on all the Web pages of the website, such as logos, the navigation bar, a placeholder for Web page title, and regions defined for content. There are two types of regions available in a template:

Editable Region: Refers to elements on individual Web pages that need to be changed for individual Web pages, for example, the content and title of a Web page. You should define at least one region as editable to add or change the main content area on individual Web pages.

Non-editable Regions: Refers to elements on a Web page that remain constant on all the Web pages of a website, for example, signature or logo of a website. Changes in the elements of a Non-editable Region of a template are globally updated on all the other associated Web pages using the templates. In the following section, you will learn to create a template from an existing Web page.

Using Blank Templates

You can create a template from an existing Hypertext Markup Language (HTML) or Active Server Pages (ASP) document, or create a template from a new blank document of Dreamweaver. After you create a template, you can insert regions in it and set template preferences, such as the color of the code you want to appear in the Code view of Dreamweaver workspace, or the template region highlight color. By the way, Dreamweaver stores all template files in the Template folder of the website with a file extension .dwt. Now you can perform the following steps to create a blank template:

1. Choose **File> New** to open the New Document dialog box. Then select **Blank Template** option from the New Document dialog box.

2. Select **HTML template** option from the Template Type section, and click **Create** button at the bottom. It opens a new, blank template in the Dreamweaver workspace.

Converting an Existing Web Page into a Template

Consider a scenario where you have made a Web page based on your requirement. Now, you want to apply the same settings of this Web page to every new Web page that you create to maintain the consistency throughout the website. In such a case, Dreamweaver allows you to convert an existing Web page into a template. Perform the following steps on your computer to create a template from an existing Web page:

1. **Open** any existing Web page that you want to use as a template. In this case, you can open the same Web page of CSS layouts which you have already created in lesson 14 (picture 5.3).

2. Choose **File> Save As** from the Menu bar. Then **browse** to the Templates folder to save this Web page as a template.

3. In File name text box, **type** the name of the template as: **first_template.dwt**, and click the **Save** button. The Dreamweaver message box appears that prompts for confirmation to update the links.

4. Click the **Yes** button of the message box. You will see that the template is created with the name **first_template**.

Working with Editable Region

The Editable Region in a template is an unlocked area, which can be edited. In other words, it implies that when you use the template in a Web page, the Editable Region of the template can be edited as per the requirements of the specific Web page. In this section of the lesson, you will learn to insert an Editable Region, and Remove an Editable Region.

Inserting an Editable Region

Editable Regions of a template are those areas of a template-based Web page whose content can be edited by a user. You can place the Editable Region anywhere on the template-based Web page. Perform the following steps to insert an Editable Region in a template:

1. **Select** the desired text or image that you want to set as an Editable Region in a template file. In our case, we select the upper-most layout (picture 5.3) from the **first_template.dwt** template file.

2. Choose **Templates> Editable Region** under the Common category in the Panel Group. It is on the right side of the Dreamweaver screen. A message box appears that prompts for your permission to convert the document into template.

3. Click the **OK** button on the message box, which opens the New Editable Region dialog box. Then, in the Name text box, **type** a name of the region as: **EditRegion1**, and click the **OK** button. You will see that the region (layout) you selected as editable is highlighted.

As you can see on your screen, the Editable Region is enclosed in a highlighted rectangular outline. This outline is displayed in the highlighting color set in the template preferences. A tab at the upper-left corner of the region displays the name of the region. In case you insert an empty Editable Region, instead of changing an Editable Region, the name of the region appears inside the region.

You can insert an Editable Region anywhere in a Web page, but if you want to make a table of layer editable, consider the following points:
- You can mark an entire table or a single cell from the table as a single Editable Region, but you cannot mark multiple table cells as a single Editable Region at a time.
- Layers and layer content are two separate elements. When you make a layer editable, you can change the position of the layer along with its content; however, making a layer's content editable allows you to change only the content of the layer, not its position.

Teach Yourself Adobe Dreamweaver CS6 – By Niranjan Jha – Published by Cromosys

Removing an Editable Region

If you have marked a region of a template as editable and want to make it non-editable in a template-based document, you need to use the Remove Template Markup command. Perform the following steps to remove an Editable Region:

1. **Choose** the Editable Region in the Dreamweaver workspace that you selected in the preceding section.

2. Select **Modify> Templates> Remove Template Markup** from the Menu bar. You will see that the Editable Region is removed from the Web page.

Working with Optional Region

An Optional Region is an area in a template that can either be displayed or hidden in a template-based document. Optional Regions are often used when a user wants to display specific content on a Web page based on a specific condition. These conditions are set in an Optional Region of the template, either as specific values or as conditional statements (such as if-else statements). There are two types of Optional Regions: Editable Optional Region and Non-editable Optional Region. In this section, you will learn to insert an Editable Optional Region and set the values of an Editable Optional Region.

Inserting an Editable Optional Region

An Editable Optional Region allows you to show or hide the region with the ability to edit the content. For example, if the Optional Region includes an image or text, the template user can decide whether to display the content or not, and can also edit the template if desired, unlike a Non-editable Optional Region, which allows you to show or hide the region without the ability to edit the content. Perform the following steps to insert and Editable Optional Region:

1. **Select** the desired text or image that you want to set as an Editable Region in a template file. In our case, we select the upper-most layout from the **first_template.dwt** template file.

2. Choose **Templates> Editable Optional Region** under the Common category in the Panel Group. It opens the New Optional Region dialog box.

3. In the Name text box, **type** the name of the region as: **OptionalRegion1**, and click the **OK** button on the New Optional Region dialog box. You will see on your screen that an Editable Optional Region is inserted on the selected layout in the Web page.

Setting Values for an Optional Region

You can set values of an Optional Region after inserting the region in a template. For example, you can specify whether to display the default setting for the content of an Optional Region, link a parameter to an existing Optional Region, or modify a template expression. Perform the following steps to set the values of an Optional Region:

1. Click the **template button** of the same Optional Region you inserted in the previous section. You are going to set the values of this button in the Web page.

2. Click the **Edit** button in the PROPERTIES inspector, which will open the New Optional Region dialog box. Select the **Advanced** tab in this dialog box.

3. Select the **Enter expression** radio button. In the Enter expression text box, type the expression as: **MAX CHAR == 10**. Then click the **OK** button. You will see on your screen that the output appears on the Web page.

Dreamweaver adds template comment tags to the code of the template file for the new Optional Region in two locations. The first is in the head section of the template file, as shown in the following code snippet:
<!-- TemplateParam name="OptionalRegion1" type="boolean" value="true" -->

The second location is where the Optional Region appears in the body section of the template file. In the Code view of the Dreamweaver workspace, additional comment tags appear, as shown in the following code snippet:
<!-- TemplateBeginIf cond="MAX CHAR == 10" --><!-- TemplateBeginEditable name="EditRegion1" -->OptionalRegion1<!-- TemplateEndEditable --><!-- TemplateEndIf -->

You can access and edit these comment tags from the Code view. Now, let's learn about Repeating Regions, which are useful when you want to repeat an object several times on a Web page. A single Repeating Region can be used multiple times on the same Web page or on multiple Web pages.

Working with Repeating Region

You can use a Repeating Region to control the layout of sections of a Web page that need to be repeated. There are two types of Repeating Regions in Dreamweaver: Repeating Region and Repeating Table. (1) A Repeating Region does not include an Editable Region by default; however, you can insert an Editable Region in the Repeating Region, if it is required. (2) A Repeating Table allows you to define a table in a Web page and create Editable Regions in the table. You can also define which rows are to be taken as a Repeating Region. In the following sections, let's learn how to work with a Repeating Region and Repeating Table in a template-based document.

Creating a Repeating Region

Normally, Repeating Regions are used with tables, but you can also define a Repeating Region for other elements of a Web page, such as an image. Perform the following steps to create a Repeating Region:

1. **Select** the region that you want to set as a Repeating Region. In our case, we select the **AP Div element** which is just below the layout that we were working on in the previous section. This AP Div element's background color is changed to purple.

2. Choose **Templates> Repeating Region** under the Common category in the Panel Group. It opens the New Repeating Region dialog box.

3. In the Name text box, **type** the name as: **RepeatRegion1**, and click the **OK** button. You will see that a Repeating Region of the specified name is inserted on the Web page. Now let's discuss how to insert a Repeating Table.

Inserting a Repeating Table

It will be good if you insert a Repeating Table in a new document. Perform the following steps to insert a Repeating Table in Dreamweaver:

1. **Open** a new document (Untitled 1), and choose **Templates> Repeating Table** under the Common category in the Panel Group. It opens Insert Repeating Table dialog box, using which you can set various properties for the table, such as number of rows and columns, cell padding and spacing, and border.

2. In the Row text box, **type** the number of rows as: **5**, and in the Column text box, **type** the number of columns as**: 5**, and click the **OK** button. A Repeating Table with the specified setting is inserted on the Web page.

Setting Tag Attributes

A Web page contains various features, such as color, fonts, and images. Whenever a new element is added on the Web page, the addition is reflected in the Code view of the Web page in the form of tags. You can allow a user to set or modify the tag attributes, such as the background color of a table in a template-based Web page. Users can modify only those attributes that are specified as editable. You can set multiple editable attributes in a template-based Web page. In this section, you learn to first make an attribute editable and then un-editable. Perform the following steps to make a tag attribute editable:

1. **Select** an element for which you want to set an editable tag attribute. In this case, you can select the same **table** you created in the preceding section.

2. Choose **Modify> Templates> Make Attribute Editable** from the Menu bar. It opens the Editable Tag Attributes dialog box.

3. Now you need to choose an attribute from the Attribute dropdown list. For this, select the **WIDTH** attribute, and **enable** (put check mark) the Make attribute editable check box. All the options regarding the selected attribute are enabled in the Editable Tag Attributes dialog box.

4. In the Label text box, **type** a name for the attribute as: **width**. Then from the Type dropdown list, select the attribute: **Text**.

5. In the Default text box, **type** an initial value as: **100%**, and click the **OK** button. You will see on your screen that the size of the table changes on the Web page. Now you can perform the following steps to make the editable tag attribute un-editable:

6. **Select** the same table, and go to **Modify> Templates> Make Attribute Editable** to open the Editable Tag Attributes dialog box.

7. **Select** the attribute that you want to make un-editable from the Attribute dropdown list. For now, you can the **WIDTH** attribute.

8. **Clear** (disable) Make attribute editable check box. All the options regarding the selected attribute are disabled in the Editable Tag Attributes dialog box. Click the **OK** button after that. As a result, the selected table on the Web page is resized and is now un-editable by template users.

Teach Yourself Adobe Dreamweaver CS6 – By Niranjan Jha – Published by Cromosys

Lesson 16
Working with Nested Templates

A nested template is a template whose design and Editable Regions are based on another template. The Editable Regions of an original or base template remain editable in the nested template. Moreover, these regions also remain editable until new template regions are inserted in these regions. Changes made to a nested template are reflected on the Web pages based o that template. When modifications are made to the base template, the changes are applied to both the nested template and to the Web pages based on the nested template.

Creating a Nested Template

You can create a nested template by saving a document based on the original template, then creating a new template of that document. Nested templates allow you to create variations in a base template. All Editable Regions of the nested template-based document depend on the nested template rather than the base template. This means that if you create an Editable Region in a base template and then create a nested template, the Editable Region appears in the document based on the nested template. So it means, you have to first create a template-based document to create a nested template. Perform the following steps to create a nested template:

1. Select **File> New** from the Menu bar to open the New Document dialog box. Then select the **Page from Template** option on the left side of the dialog box.

2. **Select** the website from the Site section containing the template you want to use. For now, you can select the **Health and Fitness** website.

3. Select the template as **first_template** from the Template for Site section. Then click the **Create** button to create a new template. A new template appears in the Document window.

4. Choose **Templates> Make Nested Template** under the Common category in Panel Group. It opens the Save As Template dialog box.

5. In Save as text box, **type** the name of the template as: **Nested_template**, and click the **Save** button. You will see on your screen that the new template named Nested_template appears and is inserted in the Template folder.

Preventing an Editable Region Passing Through a Nested Template

While working with a nested template in Dreamweaver, the Editable Region of the main template remains editable in the nested template. A developer may want to lock all or a part of an Editable Region to prevent it from being edited by other users. The Editable Region remains editable in the nested template but becomes un-editable in Web pages based on the nested template. Therefore, it is the developer who decides whether to lock the entire Editable Region or a part of the Editable Region.
In nested templates, Editable Regions have a blue border. You can insert a template markup inside an Editable Region so that a nested template does not pass through as an Editable Region in documents based on the base template. Such regions have an orange border instead of a blue border. To prevent an Editable Region passing through a nested template, it should contain at least two Editable Regions. Perform the following steps to prevent and Editable Region to pass through a nested template:

1. **Create** two Editable Regions in the **first_template** which is your <u>base</u> template. Then choose **File> Save** to save the changes. It opens the <u>Update Template Files</u> dialog box prompting for the permission to update the changes made in the base template in the nested template as well.

2. Click the **Update** button to open the <u>Update Pages</u> dialog box. Then click the **Close** button on this dialog box.

3. Click the **Nested_template.dwt** tab at the <u>top</u> of the Dreamweaver screen to view the nested template. Then click the Editable Region named **EditRegion1** in the Nested_template.dwt document.

4. Click the **Code** tab which is at the <u>top left</u> corner below File tab in the Dreamweaver screen. The Code view appears in the Dreamweaver workspace.

5. In the Code view, **add** the following syntax to the Editable Region code:
@@("")@@

6. Click the **Design** tab at the top left corner of the screen to view the Editable Region. You will see on your screen that the Editable Region appears with an orange border.

Modifying Templates

When you make any changes on a template and save the changes, all the documents based on that template are updated automatically. You can use the Templates category of the ASSETS panel to manage existing templates. You can perform various tasks with the ASSETS panel with regard to templates, such as create a template, edit and update a template, or remove a template from a template-based Web page. Although Dreamweaver checks the syntax of a template when you save the template, it is a good idea to check the template syntax manually while editing the template.

Renaming a Template

When you add a template, it appears with the default name. However, you can rename the template according to your requirement. Perform the following steps to rename a template:

1. On the same screen (of preceding section), click **ASSETS** tab in Panel Group. Then click the **Templates** category on the left side of the <u>ASSETS panel</u>, as shown in picture 5.4 with the red arrow.

2. Select the template **Untitled-1** to rename. Then you need to **right-click** the Untitle-1 template to open the <u>context menu</u>.

3. In the context menu, select the **Rename** option. A text box appears around the name Untitled-1 in the ASSETS panel.

4. **Type** a new name for the selected template. For now, you type the name as: **Sample_template**. Then press the **Enter** key on the keyboard to save the template with the new name. The new name of the template appears in the ASSETS panel.

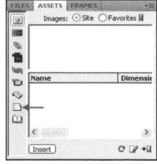

Picture 5.4

Editing an Existing Template

You can either open a template file directly from the Template folder in the ASSETS panel or open a template-based document that consists the template that you want to edit. When you make a change to a template file, Dreamweaver prompts you to update the documents based on the template. Perform the following steps to edit a template:

1. Select the **first_template** template that you will edit. Then click the **Edit** button at the bottom of the ASSETS panel, as shown in picture 5.5 with the red arrow. It opens the first_template template in the Dreamweaver workspace.

2. To select the region where you want to make changes, select the **AP Div element**. Then click the **Browse for File** icon in the PROPERTIES panel (in the middle, next to Bg image option). It opens the Select Image Source dialog box.

3. **Browse** to the location where you have an (any) image file. Then **select** the image and click the **OK** button. A message box appears prompting you to copy the image to the root folder.

Picture 5.5

4. Click the **Yes** button on the message box. It opens the Copy File As dialog box. Then **type** the name of the image as: **image1**, and click the **Save** button. You will see on your screen that the image1 image is inserted in the AP Div element you had selected.

5. Choose **File> Save** to save the changes. As the changes are made to the base template, the Update Template File dialog box appears that prompts to update the changes to the nested template as well.

6. Click the **Update** button on the Update Template File dialog box. It opens the Update Pages dialog box. Then click the **Close** button to close the Update Pages dialog box. The changes are saved and applied to the **first_template** template.

Deleting a Template

You can delete a template file from a template-based website. However, remember that the template file, once deleted, cannot be retrieved again. In other words, the template file is deleted permanently from the website. Perform the following steps to delete a template:

1. Select the **Nested_template** template that you will delete. Then click the **Delete** button at the bottom of the ASSETS panel. This Delete button is just beside the Edit button. A message box prompts you for the confirmation to delete the template.

2. Click the **Yes** button on the message box. You will see that the **Nested_template** template is deleted from the ASSETS panel.

Documents based on a deleted template file are not detached from the template; they still retain the structure and Editable Region that the template file had before its deletion. You can convert such documents into an HTML files without editable or locked regions.

Teach Yourself Adobe Dreamweaver CS6 – By Niranjan Jha – Published by Cromosys

Applying a Template to an Existing Web Page

When you apply a template to a Web page that already contains content, Dreamweaver attempts to match the existing content to a region in the template. If you are applying a revised version of one of the existing templates, the names are likely to match. Dreamweaver compresses the names of the Editable Regions in the Web page to the names of the Editable Regions in the new template; for each region name that matches, Dreamweaver places the existing content of that region into the new region with the same name. If you apply a template to a Web page that hasn't had a template applied to it, there are not Editable Regions to compare and a mismatch occurs. You can apply a template to an existing Web page by using the ASSETS panel or from the Web page. Perform the following steps to apply a template to an existing Web page:

1. **Create** a new Web page on which you want to apply the template. Then select **Sample_template** template in the ASSETS panel.

2. Click the **Apply** button at the bottom of the ASSETS panel. As a result, the data of the selected template is copied to the Web page.

Detaching a Template from a Web Page

You can make changes to the locked regions of a template-based Web page by detaching the template from a Web page. When the Web page is detached, it becomes editable, and you can make changes to it according to your requirement. Perform the following steps to detach a template from the Web page:

1. **Open** the Web page from which you want to detach the template. In this case, you can open the **Untitled-1** Web page which you created in the preceding section.

2. Choose **Modify> Templates> Detach from Template**. As a result, the Web page is detached from the template and all the code related to the template is removed.

Exporting a Template-Based Website

Dreamweaver provides you the facility to export data of a template-based website to XML files so that the data can be applied to a new template. Dreamweaver allows you to export an entire template-based website to a new folder on your computer without any template markup code. In this way, you can easily modify or update the template and add it to the exported website. Here are the steps to export a template-based website:

1. **Open** a template file (**first_template**), and choose **Modify> Export without Markup**. It opens the Export Site Without Template Markup dialog box.

2. Click the **Browse** button to select a folder for exporting the website. It opens the Extract template XML dialog box.

You should select a folder other than the current local site folder for the exported template-based website. In addition, always keep the original files of the template-based website in the local folder, as these files contain the template markup code that can be used for updating the template in the template-based website in the future.

Teach Yourself Adobe Dreamweaver CS6 – By Niranjan Jha – Published by Cromosys

3. Browse to the location as **Desktop** (not Dreamweaver CS6 folder), and click the **Select** button at the bottom. The URL of the selected location appears in the Folder text box.

4. Click the **OK** button on dialog box. It opens the **File-Activity – Extracting template XML** message box. This message box is closed automatically after sometime, and all the files are extracted on Desktop.

Exploring Library Items
Library items refer to elements that are repeatedly used in a website, such as banners and logos. After the creation of these library items, you can use instances of these library items as you want in a website. You can simply use the ASSETS panel whenever you need to insert a library item on a Web page. So in this section, you will learn to create a library item, insert a library item, and edit a library item.

Creating a Library Item
Consider a scenario, where you want to insert the copyright information to every single Web page of a website. Creating this element repetitively for every Web page is a tedious task. In such case, you can create this element as a library item and then insert it in every Web page form the ASSETS panel. You can perform these steps to create a library item:

1. **Open** a Web page (**Articles.html**) where the element that you want to make as a library item is placed. Then **select** the element on the Web page that you want to create as a library item. For now, you can select the **© ALL RIGHTS RESERVED** text.

2. Choose **Modify> Library> Add Object to Library**. The library item is created in the ASSETS panel. Then **type** the name of the library item as: **LibraryItem1**, and press the **Enter** key. As a result, the library item appears in the ASSETS panel with the specified name.

Inserting a Library Item
Dreamweaver allows you to insert any library item in a page to avoid having to recreate it. Multiple instances of the same element can be inserted on the required Web page in a short span of time. Perform these steps to insert a library item:

1. **Open** the Web page (**Untitled-1**) where you want to insert the library item. Then **select** the place to insert the library item.

2. **Select** the **LibraryItem1** library item, and click the **Insert** button. As a result, the library item is inserted in the Web page.

Editing a Library Item
When an instance of library item is inserted in a Web page, they are locked and cannot be edited. In case you want to edit the library item, first you need to unlock it and make changes to a library item. When the changes are made, all the instances are updated automatically. This feature of the Dreamweaver, application allows you to make changes globally and helps you to save time during the process of updating and redesigning the website. Perform the following steps to edit a library item:

1. **Select** the **LibraryElement1** library item from the ASSETS panel, and click the **Edit** button. It opens the **LibraryItem1.lbi** file on the Dreamweaver screen.

2. **Make** the desired changes (add some text) to the library item. Then select **File> Save** to save the changes. It opens the Update Library Items message box.

3. Click the **Update** button in the message box which opens the Update Pages window. Then click the **Close** button.

You can view the changes by opening any other Web page where the specific library item is used. For this, you can open the Articles.html Web page by clicking the Articles.html tab.

Lesson 17
Working with Spry and JavaScript

You can create simple and complex websites using Dreamweaver. A simple website can be created using Hypertext Markup Language (HTML); however, in case of complex websites, you need to use various other languages, such as Cascading Style Sheets (CSS) and JavaScript, to give your website a professional look. An ideal website is the one that is interactive, user-friendly, and easy to use. Dreamweaver allows you to create interactive websites by using the Spry widgets and behaviors in a website. You can add these widgets and behaviors in the Web pages from the Spry menu and Behavior panel.

JavaScript is a scripting language that helps to enhance static Web pages by allowing you to add interactive elements, such as flashy dropdown menus, dynamic slide shows, and moving text. The main reason for choosing JavaScript over any other scripting languages is that it is supported by all major browsers, such as Internet Explorer, Mozilla Firefox, and Opera. JavaScript is a client-side scripting language, which implies that you can interact with a Web page containing JavaScript even when you are not connected to the Internet. You can create JavaScript code for a Web application using any text editor, such as Notepad, and run it into a browser. You can also use JavaScript with a Web designing tool, such as Dreamweaver to create interactive Web pages. In Dreamweaver, JavaScript code is written in the HTML editor.

In this and next lessons, you explore Spry behaviors, including how to create and edit a dropdown menu. In addition, you learn how to use the Open Browser Window behavior. You will also be introduced with JavaScript behaviors and you will learn to create, modify, and delete these behaviors in Dreamweaver. At the end, you will also learn to use JavaScript to add interactivity to Web pages, such as displaying alert and confirm boxes, detecting browsers, creating dynamic slide shows, alerting the contents between two frames, and validating forms.

Introducing Spry Behaviors

Behaviors refer to the events that result from cause and effect relationships. Consider a scenario where you use the rollover image in a Web page. In such case, placing the mouse-pointer on the image is a cause and the change of image that occurs by placing the mouse-pointer over the image is the effect of the cause. Dreamweaver allows you to add various types of Spry behaviors, such as Spry Validation Radio Group and Spry Validation Confirm. In this section, you learn to create a dropdown, and Edit a dropdown.

Creating a Dropdown Menu

Using Dreamweaver's Spry widgets, you can add interactive behaviors to make a Web page alluring and user-friendly. Dropdown menu is the most commonly used Spry widget that can be added to a Web page. It consists of a dropdown list of the hyperlinks that enable you to easily navigate throughout the website as well as within the Web page. Perform the following steps to create a dropdown menu:

1. **Open** a Web page (Articles.html) where you want to create the dropdown menu. Then **click** at the required place where you want to place the dropdown menu.

2. **Click** the down arrow icon present in the INSERT panel in the Panel Group. Then select the **Spry** option. It opens the options present in the Spry menu.

3. Select the **Spry Menu Bar** option, as shown in picture 5.6 with the red arrow. It opens Spry Menu Bar dialog box where you can select a layout, horizontal or vertical, for appearance of the dropdown menu.

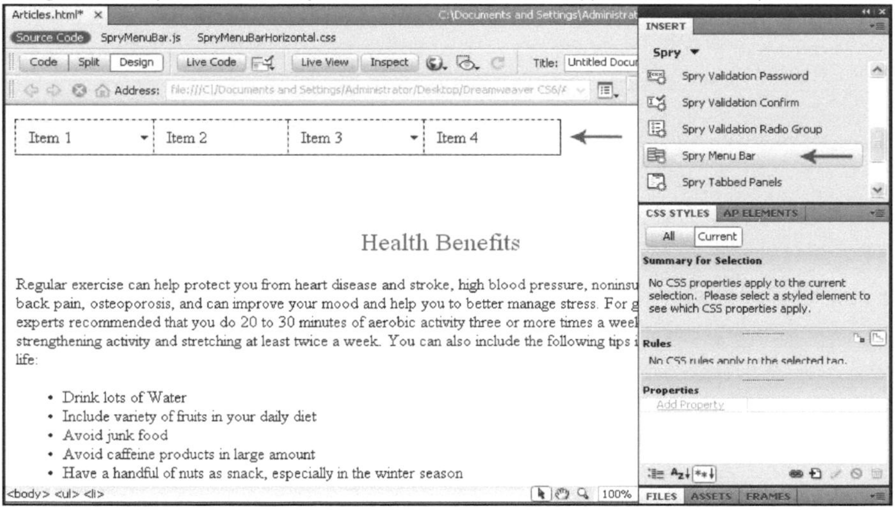

Picture 5.6

4. Select the **Horizontal** layout, and click the **OK** button. As a result, the Spry Menu is created in the Web page, as shown in picture 5.6.

5. In the PROPERTIES inspector, select the **Item 1** to rename it, as shown in picture 5.7 with the first red arrow from the left. *Click on blue label above boxes*

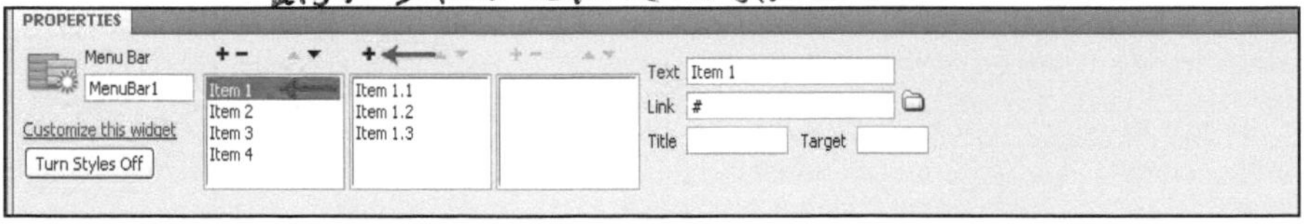

Picture 5.7

Teach Yourself Adobe Dreamweaver CS6 – By Niranjan Jha – Published by Cromosys

6. In the Text option box which is on the right side in the PROPERTIES inspector, **type** the name of Item 1 as: **Articles**.

7. **Repeat** steps 5 and 6 to rename other items, depending on your requirement. If you want, you can rename all the items of the Spry Menu.

8. **Select** the item to which you want to add sub-item from the PROPERTIES inspector. For now, you can select **Articles** item, and click the **Add menu item (+)** icon, as shown in picture 5.7 with the second red arrow from the left. The **Untitled Item** sub-item appears.

9. **Repeat** step 8 to add more sub-items to the Articles item depending on your requirement. You can also delete the items and sub-items that you do not require in the Spry Menu Bar. To delete, you can select the item or sub-item, and click the **Remove menu item (-)** icon.

Editing a Dropdown Menu

After the addition of the dropdown menu, it might be possible that you want to customize it according to the layout of your website, to maintain the consistency throughout. For example, you can change the font properties, such as size, style, and color, of the items in the menu according to your requirement. Perform the following steps to edit a dropdown menu:

1. Double-click the required style from the **CSS STYLES** panel in the Panel Group that you want to edit. In our case, we select the **ul.MenuBarHorizontal** style, as shown in picture 5.8 with the red arrow. It opens the **CSS Rule Definition for ul.MenuBarHorizontal in SpryMenuBarHorizontal.css** dialog box.

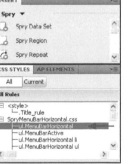

2. **Select** the desired family of font from the Font-family list box. For now, you can select the **Comic Sans MS, cursive** font family.

3. **Click** the down arrow of the Color box which opens the color palette. Then select the **blue** color and click the **OK** button.

4. Select **File> Save** to save the changes. The Dreamweaver dialog box appears that prompts you to update the links.

Picture 5.8

5. Click the **Yes** button to update the links. Then select File> Preview in Browser> IExplore to preview the Web page in Internet Explorer. The Web page appears in the browser with the modified font family and background color.

Using the Open Browser Window Behavior

Dreamweaver allows you to launch a new Web browser window when you click a hyperlink. In addition to the launch of a Web browser window, you can also specify the height and width of the Web browser considering the inserted image or video. Perform the following steps to use the Open Browser Window behavior:

Teach Yourself Adobe Dreamweaver CS6 – By Niranjan Jha – Published by Cromosys

1. **Select** the text of image that you want to set as a hyperlink. For now, you can select the **image** present on the **Tips.html** Web page.

2. Choose **Window> Behaviors** to open the Behaviors panel in the Panel Group. Then click the button **Add Behavior (+)** which is just below the Behaviors tab in the Panel Group. It opens a dropdown list.

3. Select the **Open Browser Window** option from the list. It opens the Open Browser Window dialog box. Then click the **Browse** button to locate the file that is to be opened. It opens the Select File dialog box.

4. **Select** the desired .html file that you want the hyperlink to open, and then click the **OK** button. The URL of the file appears in the URL to display text box.

5. In the Window width text box, **type** the value for width as: **500**. Then in the Window height text box, type the value for height as: **650**. And then click the **OK** button.

6. Choose **File> Save** to save the changes. Then go to **File> Preview in Browser> IExplore** to preview the Web page in Internet Explorer.

7. **Click** the image in the browser. As a result, the linked html page opens in a new window with the specified width and height.

Introducing JavaScript Behaviors

Whenever you interact with a Web page, certain events occur, such as mouse-click, mouse-over, Web page loading, image loading, and keystrokes. A Web page may contain various events associated with different page elements, such as a mouse-click event that is generated when you click a button; whereas, an image loading event is generated when you place the mouse-pointer over a graphic. The combination of an event with an action triggered by that event is known as a JavaScript behavior. The generation of an event is accompanied by an action. It means that every time an event is generated, JavaScript performs an action, such as opening a Web page or loading an image. A JavaScript behavior is a client-side JavaScript code that runs in Web browsers and not on servers. Let's first learn to work with the JavaScript behaviors contained in the Behaviors panel of Dreamweaver.

Working With the Behavior Panel

The Behaviors panel in Dreamweaver helps to insert various JavaScript behaviors and modify parameters of previously attached behaviors in a Web page. In Dreamweaver, you can add behaviors to a Web page by specifying an action and an event to trigger that action. When you attach a behavior to a Web page element, JavaScript generates an event associated with that Web page element. The behaviors that are already attached to the currently selected page elements appear in the behavior list of the Behaviors panel. If several actions are specified for the same event, then the actions execute in the order in which they are specified in the list. The following are the options available in the Behavior panel:

Show set events: Displays only those events that are attached to the current Web page.
Show all events: Displays an alphabetical list of events for a given category.

Add behavior (+): Displays a list of JavaScript actions that can be attached to the selected element.
Remove event (-): Deletes the selected event and the associated action from the behavior list.
Move event value up/down: Moves the selected action up and down in the behavior list for a particular event. This helps you to change the order of actions in the behavior list.

Working with behaviors in JavaScript includes inserting new behaviors and editing the parameters of the existing behavior. So in this part of the lesson, you will learn to add a behavior, modify a behavior, and delete a behavior.

Adding a Behavior

Dreamweaver allows you to add JavaScript behaviors to the Web page elements. These behaviors can be found under the Behaviors panel. You can attach a behavior to an entire Web page, text, graphic, and other Web page elements. A hyperlink is created when you attach a behavior to the Web page element. When you click that hyperlink, it generates an event. Perform the following steps carefully to add a JavaScript behavior to the Web page element:

1. **Create** new or open an existing page. In our case, we open a previously created **Water.html** Web page.

2. **Select** the page element to set the behaviors in the Web page. For this, you can select a **text** (any text) of the page.

3. In the Link text box of the PROPERTIES inspector, type **JavaScript:;** to create a null hyperlink on the selected text.

4. Click the **Add behavior (+)** button in the Behaviors panel in the Panel Group. It opens a list of actions on the Dreamweaver screen.

5. Select the **Call JavaScript** option from the list of actions to open the Call JavaScript dialog box. Then **type** the required JavaScript code or function in the dialog box. For now, type the **window.close();** function.

6. Click the **OK** button in the dialog box. Then choose **File> Save** to save the changes. And then go to File> **Preview in Browser> IExplore** to preview the Web page in Internet Explorer.

7. **Click** the text that you had selected for setting the behavior. It will run the JavaScript function and the **Windows Internet Explorer** message will appear on the screen. You can click the **Yes** button to close the message box.

Modifying a Behavior

Sometimes you might realize that the behavior you have created in the website is not the same you want. In such case, Dreamweaver allows you to modify the existing behavior. After attaching JavaScript behavior to the Web page element, you can modify it by changing the event associated with the Web page element. Perform the following steps to modify a behavior:

1. **Click** the same text element to which you have attached the behavior in the previous section. Then you need to **right-click** the Call JavaScript event from the list of events in the Behaviors panel in the Panel Group. It opens the context menu.

2. Select the **Edit Behavior** option in the context menu to open the Call JavaScript dialog box. Then type a new JavaScript **window.open();** function.

3. Click the **OK** button in the dialog box. Then choose **File> Save** to save the changes. And then go to **File> Preview in Browser> IExplore** to preview the Web page in Internet Explorer.

4. **Click** the text to run the JavaScript function. As a result, it will open a new Internet Explorer window on the screen.

Deleting a Behavior
Sometimes you might encounter a behavior in a Web page that you do not require any more. In such case, Dreamweaver allows you to delete the behavior. You can perform the following steps to delete a behavior:

1. **Right-click** the **Call JavaScript** event from the list of events in the Behaviors panel. It opens the context menu on the screen.

2. Click the **Delete Behavior** option. The selected behavior is deleted. Then choose File> Save to save the changes.

Lesson 18
Adding JavaScript to a Web Page
JavaScript is a scripting language that helps you to create interactive Web pages, such as pages that can verify user input, store information, and process decisions based on conditions. It enables you to access as well as manage all the components that make up a Web page. In this lesson, you will learn to display an alert message, display a confirm box, and detect browsers.

Displaying an Alert Box
The alert box displays a message to the user and requires an acknowledgement (by clicking the OK button) that the message has been read by the user. It is used to provide simple confirmation to an action by the user. The alert () method of JavaScript displays an alert box in the Web page. The syntax to display an alert box is: alert ("text");. You can perform the following steps on your computer to display an alert box:

1. **Create** a new Web page, and click the **Code** tab to switch to the Code view. The Code view appears on the screen.

2. **Type** the code, given in **Listing 18.1** below, between the <head> and </head> tags in the Code view on your Dreamweaver screen.

Teach Yourself Adobe Dreamweaver CS6 – By Niranjan Jha – Published by Cromosys

Listing 18.1: Showing the Code to Display an Alert Box

```
Displaying an Alert box
<script type="text/javascript">
function disp_alert()
{
alert("This is an alert box! !");
}
</script>
```

In Listing 18.1, the disp_alert() function contains the code to create an alert box. The message written in the alert () method appears in the alert box. After applying the preceding code, the Web page appears, as shown in picture 5.9.

Picture 5.9

3. **Type** the code, given in **Listing 18.2**, between the <body> and </body> tags in the Code view on your Dreamweaver screen.

Listing 18.2: Showing the Code to Perform the Function on Click of a Button

```
<input type="button" onclick="disp_alert()" value="Display alert box" />
```

In Listing 18.2, we have created a button, Display alert box. When you click the Display alert box button, JavaScript generates the onclick event, which calls the disp_alert function and displays an alert box with the message, This is an alert box!!. After applying the code of Listing 18.2, the Web page appears, as shown in picture 6.0 with the red arrow at the bottom.

Picture 6.0

4. Click the **Refresh** button, as shown in picture 6.0 with the red arrow at the top. Then choose **File> Save** to save the Web page. **Type** the name of the file as: **Alert box**, and click the **Save** button. The Web page is saved with the name, **Alert box.html**.

5. Choose **File> Preview in Browser> IExplore** to preview the Web page in the Internet Explorer. Then click the **Display alert box** button. The alert box appears on the screen. You can click the **OK** button to close the alert box.

Displaying a Confirmation Box
In Web programming, a confirmation box is a box that prompts for the confirmation of a command, before executing it, given by the user. Suppose you have selected a file to delete it and pressed the delete button. In such case, before deleting the file, a confirmation box appears containing the OK and Cancel button, prompting you for the confirmation of your action. If you press the OK button, the selected file is deleted, and if you press the Cancel button, the Delete command is nulled. Note that once a confirmation box appears, you cannot proceed further until you have selected either OK button or the Cancel button.

The confirm() method is used to display a confirmation box. This method returns true if the OK button is clicked, and false if the Cancel button is clicked. The syntax to display a confirmation box is: confirm("text");. Perform the following steps to display a confirmation box:

1. **Create** a new Web page, and **type** the code given in **Listing 18.3**, between the <head> and </head> tags in the Code view.

Listing 18.3: Showing the Code to Display a Confirmation Box
Displaying Confirmation Box

```
<script type="text/javascript">
function disp_confirm()
{
var r=confirm("Press a button");
if (r==true)
    {
    document.write("You pressed OK !");
    }
else
    {
    document.write("You pressed Cancel !");
    }
}
</script>
```

After typing the preceding code given in Listing 18.3, the Web page on your screen appears, as shown in picture 6.1.

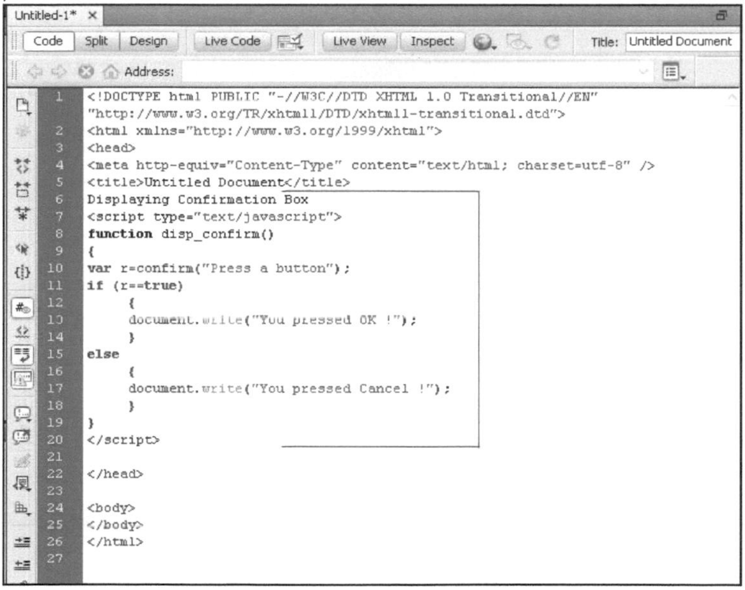

Picture 6.1

2. **Type** the code, given in **Listing 18.4**, between the <body> and </body> tags in the Code view on your Dreamweaver screen. After typing the code given in Listing 18.4, the Web page appears as shown in picture 6.2.

Listing 18.4: Showing the Code to Perform a Function on the Click of a Button
<input type="button" onclick="disp_confirm()" value="Display a confirm box" />

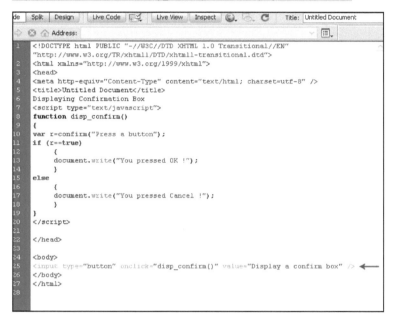

Picture 6.2

3. Click the **Refresh** button which is at the top of the Code view screen. Then choose **File> Save** to save the Web page. **Type** the name of the file as: **Confirmation box**, and click the **Save** button. The Web page is saved with the name, **Confirmation box.html**.

4. Choose **File> Preview in Browser> IExplore** to preview the Web page in Internet Explorer. Then click the **Display a confirm box** button. The **Message from webpage** dialog box appears on the screen.

5. Click the **OK** button in the dialog box. As a result, the Web page opens with the message, **You pressed OK!**

Detecting Browsers
The prime reason to detect the visitor's browser type and version is to ensure the compatibility between the browser and the website. This helps in using all the functionalities of the website. JavaScript contains an object, called Navigator, to detect the visitor's browser type and version. The JavaScript

Navigator object contains all information about the visitor's Web browser. There are two types of properties of the Navigator object: (1) **appName:** Contains the name of Web browser. (2) **appVersion:** Contains the version of Web browser. Perform the following steps to detect a visitor's browser:

1. **Create** a new Web page, and **type** the code, given in **Listing 18.5**, between the <body> and </body> tags in the Code view, as shown in picture 6.3.

Listing 18.5: Showing the Code to Detect a Browser

```
<script language="Javascript">
var browser = navigator.appName;
var version = navigator.appVersion;

alert(browser + " " + version);

if (browser.indexof("Internet Explorer") > -1) {
    document.write("Go to www.microsoft.com to download the latest browser version");
} else {
    document.write("Go to www.netscape.com to download the latest browser version");
}
</script>
<noscript>
</noscript>
```

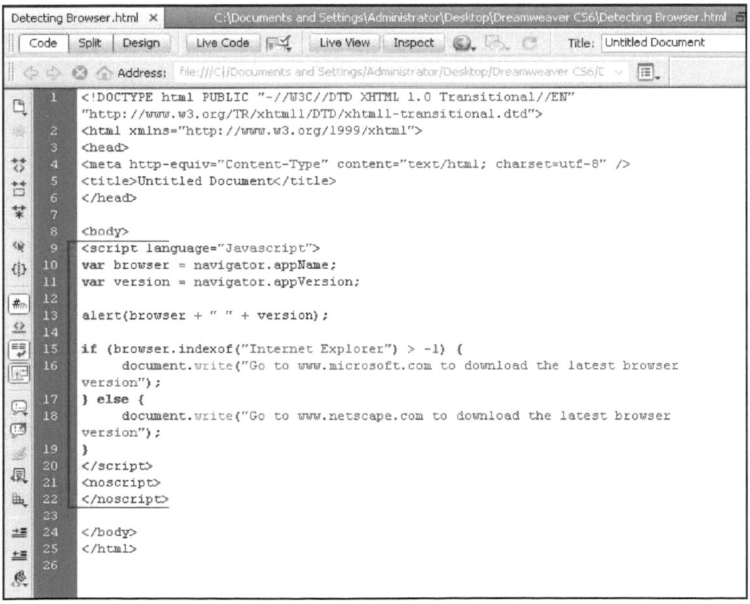

Picture 6.3

2. Click the **Refresh** button which is at the top of the Code view screen. Then choose **File> Save** to save the Web page. **Type** the name of the file as: **Detecting Browser**, and click the **Save** button. The Web page is saved with the name, **Detecting Browser.html**.

3. Choose **File> Preview in Browser> IExplore** to preview the Web page in Internet Explorer. The Internet Explorer window appears with an alert box. The alert box displays browser version and browser name.

4. Click the **OK** button in the dialog box. As a result, the Internet Explorer displays a message box on the screen.

Lesson 19
Managing, Testing, and Publishing a Website
Before publishing your website on the Internet, you need to review its content for accessibility issues, spelling errors, broken links, browser compatibility, and problems of code syntax. You can follow certain general testing guidelines so that your website is error-free and works properly on the Internet. You can test your website in different Web browser, such as Internet Explorer, Firefox, Netscape, and Opera, by using the browser compatibility feature of Dreamweaver. It is difficult to create a website that has no browser compatibility issues or occasional broken links. Therefore, testing the website helps you to indentify such issues so that you can publish a professional and user friendly website on the Internet.

Dreamweaver offers several tools that help you test your website before publishing it on the Internet. These include tools that enable you to review the content and make necessary modifications in a Web page. In addition, the Result panel of Dreamweaver includes several website evaluation tools that you can use to streamline problems related to the testing of the website.

Exploring Browser Compatibility
If you have tried to use different Web browser to browse your website, you probably must have noticed that the website appears different in each of the Web browsers. This is because the display setting of a Web page on a Web browser varies according to browser compatibility. The browser compatibility is the ability of the Web browser to interpret Hypertext Markup Language (HTML), which is used to render Web pages. HTML is a coding language that is understood differently by each Web browser. Most websites are designed to look correct in Microsoft Internet Explorer because it is the most commonly used Web browser. However, if you are a Web designer, your task is to ensure that a website is compatible with most of the Web browsers so that the Web pages can be viewed properly in other popular Web browsers as well, such as Firefox, Netscape, and Opera.

Apart from the difference in Web browsers, another factor that plays an important role in browser compatibility is whether the user is using a standard PC with the Windows, Linux, or Mac platform. The same browser renders the Web pages a little differently for each of these platforms. Dreamweaver provides the browser compatibility feature, which you can use to test a website in one or more Web browsers and generate a report. This report highlights the problems related to the appearance of the Web page of the website. In this lesson, you learn to perform the browser compatibility check, and test a Web page.

Performing the Browser Compatibility Check

You can open and view a Web page or website created in Dreamweaver across different Web browsers to check the compatibility of a Web page or website with different Web browsers, such as Internet Explorer, Firefox, Netscape, and Opera. The browser compatibility feature helps you to detect errors in the code of the website that occur during design time. A brief description of these errors is provided in the BROWSER COMPATIBILITY panel of Dreamweaver. Now perform the following steps to check a Web page by using the browser compatibility feature:

1. **Open** a Web page for which you want to perform the browser compatibility check. In our case, we open the **Tips.html** Web page.

2. Select **File> Check Page> Browser Compatibility** from the Menu bar. It displays a message: **No issues detected** at the bottom left side of the BROWSER COMPATIBILITY panel, as shown in picture 6.4.

The BROWSER COMPATIBILITY panel opens below the PROPERTIES inspector. As is obvious from the message, the Web page contains no compatibility issues. Now let's learn how to test a website in a specific Web browser in Dreamweaver.

Testing a Web Page

Dreamweaver provides you various options to test a Web page on different Web browsers. You can use these options to check your Web page or website for compatibility issues, such as the layout and color of the Web page. Perform the following steps on your computer to test a Web page in a specific Web browser:

1. **Open** the desired (Tips.html) Web page. Then click the **Options** button of the BROWSER COMPATIBILITY, as shown in picture 6.4 with the red arrow. It opens a context menu.

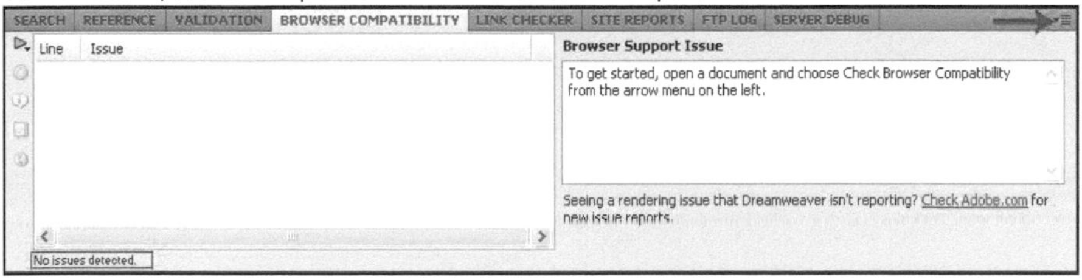

Picture 6.4

2. Select the **Settings** option from the context menu. It opens the Target Browsers dialog box. By default, all the Web browsers versions are selected.

3. **Select** the desired browser versions that you want to use to test the Web page. In our case, we select **Firefox 1.5** and **Internet Explorer 6.0**.

4. Click the **OK** button in the dialog box. The Target Browser dialog box closes. The message: **"No issues detected"** appears at the bottom of the BROWSER COMPATIBILITY panel.

Managing Links

A website is a collection of inter-connected files, such as Web pages, graphics, and Flash movies. These files are connected to each other through links. A link refers to a word, phrase, or image that you can click to navigate to a new Web page or a new section within the current Web page. Sometimes links might break when the paths they reference are not correct. In Dreamweaver, a broken link may occur due to any one of the following reason: (1) Deleting a file from a website. (2) Moving a Web page or graphic outside the website. (3) Typing an incorrect path of a file. In the following sections, you learn to fix broken links as well as update links.

Fixing Broken Links

You can fix a broken link manually on every Web page. However, this is not always practical or feasible. An alternative is to use Dreamweaver's Check Links Sitewide feature, which automatically detects and fixes broken links in the entire website. Perform the following steps to fix the broken link in a website:

1. **Open** the desired (Tips.html) Web page, and choose **Site> Check Links Sitewide** from the Menu bar. It opens the **LINK CHECKER** panel below the PROPERTIES inspector.

This panel displays the broken links that appear in the website. In our case, the People Welfare.html and the blank.jpg broken links are fond in the **Tips.html** Web page.

2. Click the **/formValidation.html** file under the Files column in the left corner of the LINK CHECKER. It opens a folder named **Browser for File** icon on the right side (under) Broken Links, as shown in picture 6.5 with the red arrow on the right side.

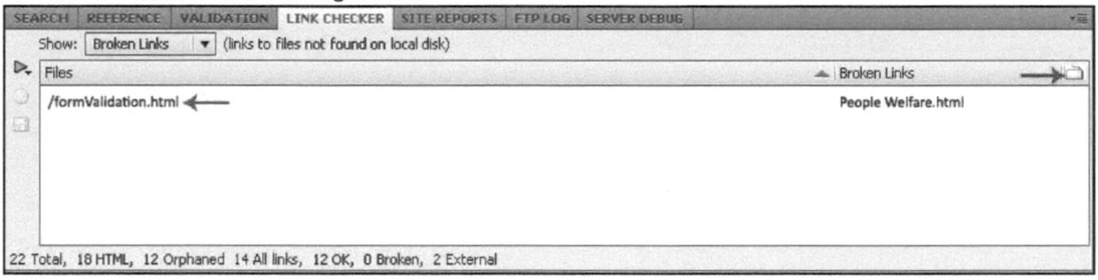

Picture 6.5

3. Click the **Browser for File** icon to fix the broken links. It opens the Select File dialog box on the Dreamweaver screen.

4. Browser to the location **Dreamweaver CS6** folder. Then select the file name: **People Welfare**, and click the **OK** button. The **People Welfare.html** broken link is fixed and does not appear in the LINK CHECKER panel.

Updating Links

Dreamweaver allows you to update links to and from a file whenever you move or rename the file within the Local folder in your computer. This feature works best when you store the website in the Local folder. Dreamweaver does not update the links in the Remote folder until you put the Local folder on or check them into the Remote folder. Perform the following steps to update a link:

1. **Select** the file whose location you want to change in the **FILES** panel. In our case, we select the **Sample_template.dwt** file.

2. **Drag** the selected file to the folder where you want to place it. In our case, we drag the selected file into the **template markup** folder. It opens the Update Files dialog box.

3. Click the **Update** button to update the link. The link in the selected file is updated and the selected file is moved to the new location.

Working with Site Management

Dreamweaver provides the Cloaking option to help you manage and organize your website. The Cloaking option in Dreamweaver enables you to exclude specific folders and files from the website. This feature is helpful if you do not want users to view a particular section of your website. For example, suppose you have a special folder that you want to make visible only during a particular time of the year (such as a special offer during festivals). In such case, you can use the Cloaking option to save the folder in your website and uncloak the folder when needed. Perform the following steps to set the Cloaking option:

1. **Open** the desired (Tips.html) Web page, and choose **Site> Manage Sites** from the Menu bar. It opens the Manage Sites dialog box.

2. **Select** the desired website. In our case, we select the **Health and Fitness** website. Then click the **Edit** button in the dialog box. The **Site Setup for Health and Fitness** dialog box appears.

3. Click the down arrow of **Advanced Settings** on the left side. It expands after you click. Then select the **Cloaking** category under the Advanced Settings tab.

4. **Select** (put check mark) the **Enable Cloaking** check box to activate the Cloaking option. Then click the Save button at the bottom.

By default, the Enable Cloaking check box is selected. You can also select the Cloak files ending with the check box to cloak specific files in the website, and specify the file extension names in the text box below this option to cloak the files containing that file extension.

Working with the Design Notes

When several people are working on a website, communication is paramount. In team collaboration, certain information needs to be communicated among all the members of the team, such as the status of a file; the dates when a file was last edited or created; what needs to be done on a file, or what has already been done; and details about images or objects, such as the source files, who created them, or where you can get additional files. Dreamweaver includes a feature called Design Notes to facilitate team communication.

Design Notes are notes you write about a file in Dreamweaver. They are associated with that file in Dreamweaver, but stored separately; therefore, they do not appear in your Web documents. A Design Note can be attached to a Web page, graphic, or media file inserted in the Web page. Design Notes follow their corresponding file whenever the file on which they are they are attached to is moved or renamed using the FILES panel. However, a Design Note is deleted when the file on which it is attached to is deleted. Design Notes have the same name as the file name to which they are attached, including the file extension, but designated with a .mno extension. These are saved in the _notes folder in the FILES panel. The Design Notes option is used to store information related to a file such as file status, comments about the file, and the name of the image source file. In this part of the lesson, you will learn to set the Design Notes option, and add Design Notes.

Setting the Design Notes Option

Before you add the Design Notes in a website, you need to set the Design Notes option to share Design Notes with others working on the website. Perform the following steps to set the Design Notes option:

1. **Open** the desired (Tips.html) Web page, and choose **Sites> Manage Sites** to open the Manage Sites dialog box on the screen.

2. **Select** the desired website. In our case, we select the **Health and Fitness**. Then click the **Edit** button. The **Site Setup for Health and Fitness** dialog box appears.

3. Click the down arrow of **Advanced Settings** to expand. Then select the **Design Notes** category under the Advanced Settings tab.

4. Click the **Clean up Design Notes** button to delete the Design Notes files that are no longer associated with the selected website. A message box appears to confirm the clean up operation.

5. Click the **Yes** button in the message box. The message box closes and the **Site Setup for Health and Fitness** dialog box reappears. Then click the **Save** button to close the dialog box.

6. The **Manage Sites** dialog box reappears on the screen. Then click the **Done** button to close the Manage Sites dialog box.

Adding Design Notes

You can add Design Note to a file after enabling the Design Notes feature in the Site Definition dialog box. A Design Note can be created for each file and template in a website. You can also create Design Notes for applets, ActiveX controls, and Flash content in a file. Perform the following steps to add a Design Note in a file:

1. **Open** the desired (Tips.html) Web page, and choose **File> Design Notes** from the Menu bar. It opens the Design Notes dialog box.

2. Click the down arrow of the **Status** option, which opens a list below. Then select the **needs attention** option.

3. Click the **Insert date** icon which is on the right side of the Status option in the dialog box. This option allows you to insert the current local date for your Design Note. After you click this icon, the current date appears in the Notes text area.

4. **Type** the text in the <u>Notes</u> text box that you want to display in the Design Notes. In our case, we type: **This file is due for modifications**. Then select the **Show when file is opened** check box so that the Design Notes file appears every time with the file it is associated.

5. Select the **All info** tab at the <u>top</u> of the Design Notes dialog box. Then click the **Plus** button to add a new key-value pair. The key-value pair denotes the values given in the Name and Value text boxes, in the All info tab. You can click the Minus button to delete a selected key-pair value.

6. Type the name: **status** in the <u>Name</u> text box for the Design Note. Then type the value: **needs attention** in the <u>Value</u> combo box. Click the **OK** button at the end.

The selected Design Notes file is saved with the Tips.html name, as the MNO file type, in the _notes folder in the same location as current file. You can view the inserted Design Notes by right-clicking the file name in the FILES panel and selecting the Design Notes option from the context menu.

Working with Website Reports
The website reports feature of Dreamweaver is used to find and fix problems related to a website before it is published on the Internet. You can create a variety of reports and even customize them to indentify website problems related to external links, redundant and empty tags, and untitled documents. The site report feature helps you to fix these and related problems. In other words, the site report feature is useful for examining, troubleshooting, and documenting a website. There are two types of site reports in Dreamweaver. (1) Those related to the workflow of the website. (2) Those related to the code of the website. You can also save and print the results of a site report. Site reports are saved in the eXtensible Markup Language (XML) file format.

Generating Website Reports
As already learned, Dreamweaver's site report feature helps you to detect and fix errors. You can generate a report for your website using this feature very easily. Perform the following steps to generate a website report:

1. **Open** the desired (Tips.html) Web page, and choose **Site> Reports** from the Menu bar. It opens the <u>Reports</u> dialog box.

2. Select the option **Current Document** from the <u>Report on</u> dropdown list. Then **select** (put check mark) all the three check boxes under the <u>Workflow</u> node. And then click the **Report Settings** button at the bottom.

It opens the <u>Recently Modified</u> dialog box on the screen. You can indicate search dates for the website report in the following two ways:
- To generate a website report on all files modified in the last several days, select the **Files Created or Modified in the Last** radio button and enter the value in the Days text box.
- To generate a website report on all files modified within a specific time frame, select the **Files Created or Modified Between** radio button, and then specify a date range.

3. For now, select the option **Files Created or Modified in the Last** radio button. Then **type** the value: **2** in the <u>Days</u> text box.

4. Click the **OK** button to close the dialog box. After you click the OK button, the Reports dialog box reappears. You need to click the **Run** button at the top in the dialog box.

The website report is generated for the Tips.html file and appears in the SITE REPORTS panel. Through the Site Reports panel you will get information regarding the HTML file and come to know what all design notes or CSS is applied in the HTML file. In case, you want to view the generated report in the Web browser, you can view it by selecting it from the root folder of your system. In our case, the path where the report gets saved is, C:\Users\Cromosys\AppData\Roaming\Adobe\DreamweaverCS6\en_US\ Configuration\Reports\Workflow\Output\TMPTeamAdmin9945.html.

Saving a Website Report
Dreamweaver allows you to save the report to be used as a reference in future, depending on the requirement. Perform the following steps to save a website report:

1. In the SITE REPORTS panel (which is below the PROPERTIES inspector), click the **Options** button, as similarly shown in picture 6.5 before. It opens the Options menu.

2. Select the **Save Results** option, which opens the Save As dialog box. Then browse to the folder **Dreamweaver CS6**.

3. Type the name as: **ResultsReport** in the File name text box. Then click the **Save** button. The Save As dialog box closes and the website report is saved in the Dreamweaver CS6 folder.

Lesson 20
Publishing a Website
Publishing is a process of uploading a website on the Web server. To upload your website on the Web server, you need to perform three steps in a sequential order. The first step is to register a domain name for your website. A domain name provides an easily recognizable name for the numerical Internet Protocol (IP) address of the website. An IP address is a numerical label assigned to devices that are connected over a network. An example of a domain name is www.adobe.com. You need to specify the domain name in the address bar of the Web browser to open a website from any individual computer. You can register a required domain name from any domain name registrar in your city.

After registering a desired domain name for your website, you need to get space on the Web hosting server. You can get space to upload your website from any Web hosting server provider for a nominal fee.

The last step is to upload the necessary files required to run the website on the server using the FTP client. It provides you a standard network protocol used to exchange files over the Web server. There are various FTP clients available in the market, such as CuteFTP. Perform the following steps to publish a website using CuteFTP:

1. Select **Start> All Programs> GlobalSCAPE> CuteFTP 8 Home** on your desktop. It opens the **Welcome to CuteFTP 8 Home!** dialog box on the screen.

2. Click the **Continue** button in the Welcome dialog box. *In case, you have a serial number to register your product, click the Enter Serial Number button.* The **Tip of the Day** dialog box appears on the screen.

3. Click the **Close** button at the bottom of the Tip of the Day dialog box. It opens the Site Manager dialog box on the screen.

4. Click the **New** dropdown list button which is at the bottom left corner. Then select the **FTP Site** option from the dropdown list to create a new FTP site. The tab related to the FTP Site option appears in the right pane of the **Site Manager** dialog box.

5. **Type** the name: **MyWebsite** in the Label text box. Type the provided host address such as: **ftp.globalscape.com**.

6. **Type** the provided username in the Username textbox or you can leave it blank. Then select the **Anonymous** radio button under the Login method.

7. Click the **Connect** button at the bottom. The hostname, username, and password are provided to you by your Web hosting service provider when you register with the Web hosting service provider.

The Connecting to Site dialog box appears on the screen. When the connection to the server is established, the **Prompt** dialog box appears.

8. Click the **OK** button in the dialog box. The **GlobalSCAPE - CuteFTP 8.0** window appears, where the host folder appears in the right panel and local folders appear in the left panel. You can drag and drop all the required files for running the website, such as HTML files, images, sound files, and CSS files, in the host folder.

100

Niranjan Jha
Cromosys Corporation
Languages and Technology Research and Education
Email: cromosys@yahoo.com
www.cromosys.in
www.facebook.com/cromosys
+91-9561450045